20 PROJECTS TO MAKE

Nursery Stitch

Rebecca Shreeve

COLLINS & BROWN

First published in the United Kingdom by Collins & Brown
10 Southcombe Street
London W14 0RA

An imprint of Anova Books Company Ltd

ISBN 978-1-90844-924-5

A CIP catalogue for this book is available from the British
Library.

10 9 8 7 6 5 4 3 2 1

Reproduction by Rival Colour Ltd, UK
Printed and bound by Toppan Leefung Printing Limited,
China

This book can be ordered direct from the publisher at
www.anovabooks.com.

Join our crafting community at LoveCrafts –
we look forward to meeting you!

Nursery Stitch

contents

introduction

Meet the menagerie! In this book you'll find a whole family of friendly animals waiting to share your child's day – from getting dressed to mealtimes, playtime, snoozetime, bathtime and bedtime. Whilst designing the projects, my aim has been to make original items that will not only be loved by children but cherished by their parents too. So often, toys and home textiles for children are brash and unsophisticated. I wanted to create a range of projects that are contemporary, yet quaint and quirky, and which will sit happily in a family home.

When it comes to selecting fabrics for the projects, it's vital to remember how delicate a baby's skin is. For garments and any home furnishings that are going to be next to the skin, such as pillow cases or comforters, use soft, natural fibres that allow the skin to breathe. Lightweight cottons (ideally organic), soft flannels and cotton fleeces are ideal. Avoid synthetic fabrics such as polyester and heavy wools that might scratch or irritate the skin. And, whatever you choose, make sure it's machine washable and quick drying. For toys, the choice of fabric is not so critical and you could use furnishing-weight cottons or even hard-wearing corduroy.

There's a bewildering choice of fabric patterns on the market, and my advice is to stick to simple patterns such as checks, spots, stripes or a simple repeat. I gather fabrics from many different places, as well as dedicated fabric shops for dressmaking and furnishing. Quilting stores sell 'fat quarters' in all kinds of wonderful patterns, which are ideal when you need only a small piece of material for an appliqué motif. Charity shops can be also a useful source of inexpensive cotton shirts and blouses, which you can then cut up and re-use.

Always wash your fabrics before you cut out the pieces and begin stitching. This minimizes the risk of shrinkage and allows you to check that the fabrics are colour fast.

Safety, of course, is paramount when it comes to making clothes and toys for babies. Little fingers have a surprisingly strong grip, and the constant gnawing and sucking of much-loved toys and comforters can loosen even the strongest stitching. So do not embellish your hand-made toys with buttons, beads, or anything else that could be pulled off and swallowed. Instead, add details with simple hand embroidery stitches.

Above all, when making toys, make sure that your seams are really firm and secure, so that no toy stuffing can come out. Work a few stitches in reverse at the start and end of each seam for security and, if seams intersect, check carefully to ensure that there are no gaps.

I feel I have put part of myself into every project; each item works well with the others, but every one is wonderfully unique. I hope you have as much fun making these projects as I did designing and creating them, and that they will be appreciated for years to come by their owners.

Rebecca Shreeve

sheep t-shirt

This T-shirt is for a two-year-old, but you can easily enlarge the sheep for any size of shirt. If you really love to sew, why not cover a whole T-shirt in sheep? The sheep would work perfectly on a tot's pyjamas – fun for counting yourself to sleep!

You will need

- Baby's T-shirt (plain colour)
- Scraps of patterned cotton fabric (body)
- Scraps of neutral (plain or patterned) cotton fabric (face and legs)
- Double-sided fusible webbing (such as Bondaweb)
- Embroidery thread (black and various colours)
- Embroidery needle
- Erasable fabric marker or iron-on transfer pen (optional)

instructions

1

Transfer the templates to the webbing: place the webbing over a template, paper side up, and trace the lines of the template. Cut out the shape roughly.

Place each shape, paper side up, on the wrong side of the appropriate fabric. Iron for 3–4 seconds (no steam).

2

Cut out the shapes accurately. Peel off the backing paper and lay the body and legs, coated side down, on the right side of the T-shirt (use the photo for guidance on positioning). The legs of each sheep should be tucked under the body piece.

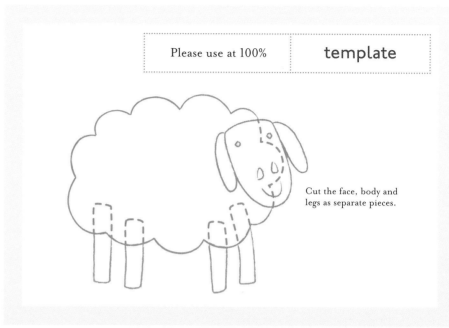

Please use at 100% | **template**

Cut the face, body and legs as separate pieces.

the sheep's face and position it on the body. Iron in place. Repeat for the other sheep and leave the motifs to cool.

horizontal stitches from one side of the leg to the other. (For details of how to work the hand stitches, see pages 108–11.)

3

Iron in place (see page 107); if the T-shirt fabric is very thin, you may need to put greaseproof paper in the middle of the shirt as a precaution to prevent the glue from the webbing seeping through to the back of the shirt. Peel off the backing paper from

4

Whipstitch around the head and body using three strands of embroidery thread and working over the edges of the motif and through the T-shirt. Make small stitches with a fairly small space between each one. Sew over each leg with a series of

5

Sew on the facial features using three strands of embroidery thread and backstitch, making French knots for the eyes. If you prefer to have a drawn line to follow, use an erasable fabric marker or an iron-on transfer pen (see page 107).

cheeky monkey socks

These socks will certainly suit your cheeky little monkey. They would also make a fabulous present for a new baby, using more subtle colours such as pale blue or pink. Alternatively, for an older child, why not enlarge the monkey and put it on slippers?

instructions

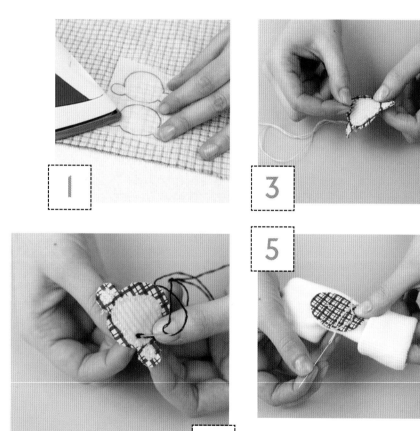

Transfer the templates to the webbing: place the webbing over a template, paper side up, and trace the lines of the template. Cut out the shape roughly, leaving a border. Place each shape, paper side up, on the wrong side of the appropriate fabric. Iron for 3–4 seconds (no steam).

2

Cut out the face and inner ear accurately. Peel off the backing paper and lay them, coated side down, on the right side of the head. Iron in place and leave to cool (see page 107).

3

Peel off the backing paper from the head. Using three strands of embroidery thread, whipstitch around the face and inner ear. (For details of how to work the hand stitches, see pages 108–11.) Make small stitches with a fairly small space between each one.

4

Backstitch the facial features, and make French knots for the eyes. If you prefer to have a drawn line to follow, use an erasable fabric marker or iron-on transfer pen (see page 107).

5

Cut out the remaining pieces accurately and peel off the backing paper. Using three strands of embroidery thread, sew a cross in the middle of the body for the tummy button.

Pin the head on the ankle cuff and the body on the foot of the sock. Whipstitch around all the pieces (as before) to attach them to the sock.

6

Add the arms, legs and tail, leaving a tiny gap between the pieces and the body. (In this project, the pieces are not fused to the sock by ironing, as this would prevent the sock from being able to stretch in wear.)

template

Please use at 100%

Cut the face, body, tail and legs as separate pieces.

bunny bib

You will need

Toddler's bib (white, plain)

Scraps of patterned cotton fabric
(rabbits' heads and bodies, legs,
carrots and apple)

Double-sided fusible webbing
(such as Bondaweb)

Tear-away fusible stabilizer
(such as Vilene Stitch 'n' Tear)

Embroidery thread (black
and red, or colour to suit)

Embroidery needle

Sewing machine with
a freehand foot

Sewing thread

Erasable fabric marker
or iron-on transfer pen
(optional)

This bib will definitely brighten up mealtimes. Although it may be hard to see it get messy after all your hard work, it washes well at a low temperature. Why not make a set of bibs, repositioning and enlarging the motifs – you could have just one big bunny, or a bib patterned in carrots.

instructions

When you buy plain bibs, they usually come in a set, so make use of them all by making a whole family of bunnies in different sizes.

Transfer the templates to the webbing: place the webbing over a template, paper side up, and trace the lines of the template. Cut out the shape roughly. (You will need six carrots – three for each side of the bib.)

Place each shape, paper side up, on the wrong side of the appropriate fabric. Iron for 3–4 seconds (no steam).

Cut out the shapes accurately. Peel off the backing paper and lay them, coated side down, on the right side of the bib (use the photo for guidance on positioning) and then iron in position and leave to cool (see pages 106–7). Fix the rabbits' bodies and apple first, then the back legs, and finally arrange the carrots up the sides of the bib.

Pin the tear-away stabilizer to the back of the bib, to cover the area behind the motifs. Tack in place.

Using the freehand foot, machine-stitch around each motif just inside the edge and to highlight details on the templates (a thread in a contrasting colour looks good). Use an embroidery hoop if you wish. Transfer template details with an iron-on transfer pen (see page 107).

Carefully pull the tear-away stabilizer from the back of the bib, making sure you remove it from inside the motifs.

6

Decorate the bib by sewing a chunky running stitch just inside the edge of the bib, all the way around, using all six strands of embroidery thread. (For details of how to work the hand stitches, see pages 108–11.)

7

Sew on the facial features using three strands of black embroidery thread and backstitch, making French knots for the rabbits' eyes and using the photo for guidance. If you prefer to have a drawn line to follow, use an erasable fabric marker or an iron-on transfer pen.

Apple

Carrot x 6

Cut the rabbits' back legs
as a separate piece.

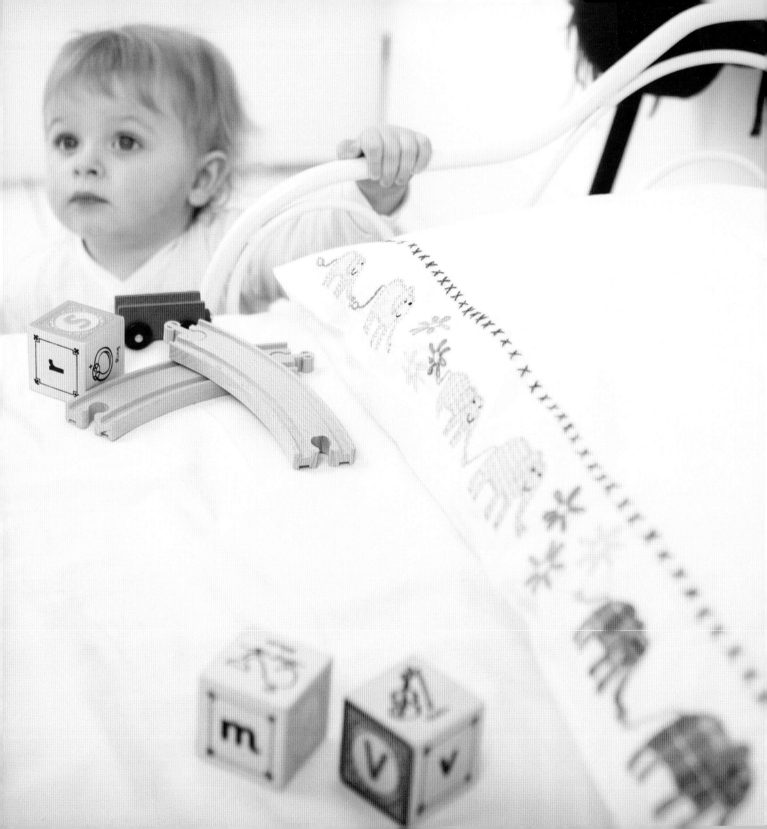

elephant pillowcase

You will need

Plain white or cream pillowcase

Scraps of patterned cotton fabric: minimum of four different kinds (elephants)

Double-sided fusible webbing (such as Bondaweb)

Embroidery thread (black and six colours)

Embroidery needle

Erasable fabric marker

Ruler or tape measure

Iron-on transfer pen (optional)

This lovely pillowcase is bound to ensure sweet dreams. Use patterns and colours that are subtle but vibrant, and which work well together. Choose bold thread colours that complement, yet stand out from, the fabric patterns.

instructions

1

On the two longer sides of the front of the pillowcase, measure 7cm (2³⁄₄in) in towards the centre. Use the fabric marker to mark a line of dots, 2cm (³⁄₄in) apart, beginning 2cm (³⁄₄in) from the edge.

2

Take one of the embroidery threads and sew a cross over each dot, working only on the front of the pillowcase, to make a row of cross-stitch with a gap between each cross. (For details of how to work the hand stitches, see pages 108–11.) (Keep checking that you are only sewing through the front of the pillowcase – keep your hand inside to prevent yourself from catching in the back by mistake.)

3

If you are using a fabric marker that has an eraser to remove the marks, rub out the dots now.

4

Transfer the templates to the webbing: place the webbing over a template, paper side up, and trace the lines of the template. Cut out the shape roughly. Make sure that you make three pairs of elephants for each end of the pillowcase, with three pairs facing to the right and three facing to the left.

Place each shape, paper side up, on the wrong side of the appropriate fabric. (It looks effective if you use a different fabric for each pair of elephants.) Iron for 3–4 seconds (no steam). Cut out the shapes accurately.

5

Using the picture for guidance, attach the elephants to one long side of the front of the pillowcase. Peel off the backing paper and lay the elephants, coated side down, under the row of cross-stitching. Leave a small gap between each big and little elephant, an equal gap between the pairs, and a small space between the end elephants and the edge of the pillowcase. Iron in place and leave to cool (see page 107). Attach the ears in the same way. Repeat at the other side of the pillowcase, with the pairs of animals walking in the opposite direction and sitting above the row of cross-stitch.

6

Using two strands of embroidery thread, whipstitch around each elephant and around its ear. Make small stitches with a fairly small space between each one. Use a different coloured thread for each fabric; a contrasting colour to the fabric looks best.

7

Create the elephants' tails by working backstitch with six strands of embroidery thread. Each big elephant's tail should reach the trunk of the little elephant behind it.

Sew on the facial features, using three strands of black embroidery thread. Make French knots for the eyes and use backstitch for the mouth. If you prefer to have a drawn line to follow, use an erasable fabric marker or an iron-on transfer pen (see page 107).

Now embroider three flowers in each gap between the elephants, using a different coloured embroidery thread for each one. Using all six strands of embroidery thread, sew a small circle consisting of seven stitches. Then make a petal at each of the seven points where the stitches meet, using lazy daisy stitch (see page 110).

Add a row of ten more flowers down the open edge of the front of the pillowcase, using the same method, working them in different colours.

11

To make a pillowcase for a boy, choose fabrics and colours that you think are suitable, and replace the flowers with a star if you wish. Draw a star shape on the fabric with an erasable fabric marker. You can either draw a five-pointed star, or make a six-pointed star by drawing two triangles on top of each other. Sew around the star shape using six strands of embroidery thread and backstitch.

12

Iron the pillowcase, put a pillow inside and it is ready to be used.

Cut the elephants' ears as a separate piece.

Please use at 100% template

Elephant Pillowcase 23

whale towel

Plain towel in a pale colour

Scraps of patterned cotton fabric (whales and water spurts)

Cotton fabric: a little wider than the width of towel x 25cm (10in) (sea background)

Double-sided fusible webbing (such as Bondaweb) (size as for sea background, plus sufficient to back whales)

Embroidery thread (black and blue)

Embroidery needle

Sewing machine with a freehand foot and a zigzag foot

Sewing thread

Erasable fabric marker

Ruler

Iron-on transfer pen (optional)

This very simple and satisfying project is a great way to jazz up a plain towel – and it will make bathtime more fun. You can adjust the pattern for a bigger towel by making the background strips longer and adding more whales – your whole family could have matching towels, all in different colours.

instructions

2

Transfer the templates for the whales and water spurts to the webbing: place the webbing over a template, paper side up, and trace the lines of the template. Cut out the shape roughly. The towel features seven whales at each end (one set facing to the left and one set facing to the right), but you may need more or fewer whales depending on the size of your towel.

3

Place each shape, paper side up, on the wrong side of the appropriate fabric. Iron for 3–4 seconds (no steam). Cut out the shapes accurately.

1

Take the fabric for the sea and draw two rectangles side by side, with a small gap between them, using the fabric marker. Make each rectangle the width of the towel x 7cm (2¾in).

4

Peel off the backing paper and arrange the whales, coated side down, on the right side of the sea background (use the photo for guidance on positioning). Position a spurt of water over each whale's head, tucking it slightly under the head. Iron in place and leave the motifs to cool (see page 107).

Place a piece of webbing, paper side up, on the wrong side of each sea background piece. Iron for 3–4 seconds (no steam) and then leave to cool. Peel off the backing paper.

5

Using the freehand foot, machine-stitch carefully around each motif just inside the edge.

6

Backstitch the whales' facial features using three strands of black embroidery thread, and make French knots for the eyes. (For details of how to work the hand stitches, see pages 108–11.) If you prefer to have a drawn line to follow, use an erasable fabric marker or an iron-on transfer pen (see page 107).

Embroider splashes around the spurts, using three strands of blue embroidery thread and working a few stitches over each other to make the shapes.

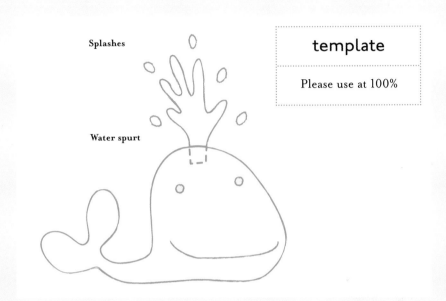

Splashes

Water spurt

template

Please use at 100%

7

Cut out each sea background: it should measure the width of the towel x 7cm (2³/₄in).

8

Position each strip of whales at each end of the towel. The base of the whales should face the edge of the towel. Iron in place and leave to cool (see page 107).

9

Machine-stitch around each strip using a zigzag foot. The towel is ready to make bathtime fun!

teddy hat

You will need

Fleece fabric: 0.5m x 147cm
($^1/_2$yd x 58in)

Scraps of patterned cotton
fabric (inner ears and muzzle)

Double-sided fusible webbing
(such as Bondaweb) (muzzle)

Embroidery thread (black and
yellow, or colours to suit)

Embroidery needle

Sewing machine

Sewing thread

Erasable marker and iron-on
transfer pen

This hat is practical as well as very cute. It will keep baby's head warm when out and about, and makes fun at-home loungewear! It will make a great present for a new baby, and the neutral colours mean it's suitable for a boy or a girl.

instructions

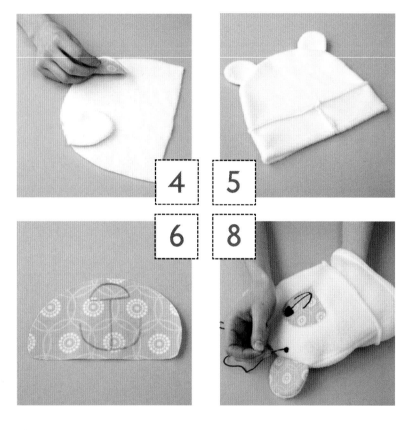

1

Use the templates to cut out the hat pieces, outer ears and band from the fleece, and inner ears from the cotton fabric. The pieces should include a seam allowance of 6mm ($\frac{1}{4}$in).

Use an erasable fabric marker to mark the positions of the ears (see pages 106–7).

2

Make the muzzle: place the webbing over the template, paper side up, and trace the lines. Cut out the shape roughly; place paper side up on the wrong side of the cotton fabric. Iron for 3–4 seconds (no steam). Cut out the muzzle accurately. Remove the backing paper.

3

Place the outer and inner ear with right sides together, pin and tack. Machine-stitch around each ear with a 6mm ($\frac{1}{4}$in) seam, leaving the base open. Cut triangular notches out of the seam allowance to reduce bulk. Turn the ears right side out and press with your fingers.

4

Lay one hat piece with right side uppermost. With raw edge to raw edge, position each ear as marked on the template, the ear lying on the hat. Pin and tack.

Place the two hat pieces with right sides together. Machine-stitch around the hat with a 6mm ($\frac{1}{4}$in) seam, sewing in the ears and leaving the base open.

5

Hem one long edge of the band. With right sides together, stitch the short ends with a 6mm ($\frac{1}{4}$in) seam. Press the seam open with your fingers. Pin the raw edge of the band to the base of the hat, right side of band to wrong side of hat. Make sure that the band's seam is at the back of the hat (inner ears are on the front of the hat). Tack and machine-stitch in place.

Use the iron-on transfer pen to transfer the nose and mouth to the muzzle. Using six strands of black embroidery thread, backstitch the line under the nose and along the mouth. (For details of how to work the hand stitches, see pages 108–11.) Embroider the nose using satin stitch.

Whipstitch the muzzle to the hat using three strands of embroidery thread. Make small stitches with a fairly small space between each one. (The motif is not ironed into position, as the heat would flatten the surrounding fleece.)

Using six strands of black embroidery thread, backstitch a circle for each eye and then fill it in using two layers of satin stitch to give a raised effect.

Fold the band to the right side of the hat to create the turn-up.

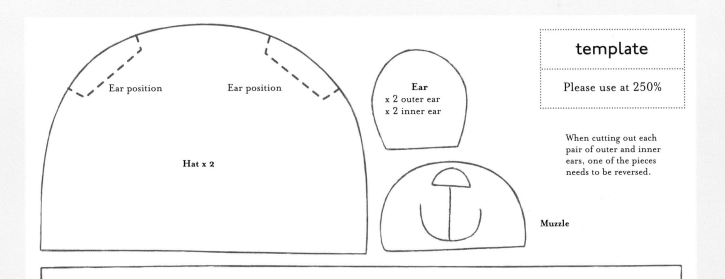

Ear position   Ear position

Hat x 2

Ear
x 2 outer ear
x 2 inner ear

template

Please use at 250%

When cutting out each pair of outer and inner ears, one of the pieces needs to be reversed.

Muzzle

Band

rabbit blankie

This gorgeous rabbit comforter blanket is going to be well loved. It is perfect for a baby, as the soft body is cosy and warm; when baby is a little older, the head is ideal for tiny hands to grip. Toddlers will adore it too. Make it as a gift for a new baby and choose fabric colours according to whether the new arrival is a girl or a boy!

instructions

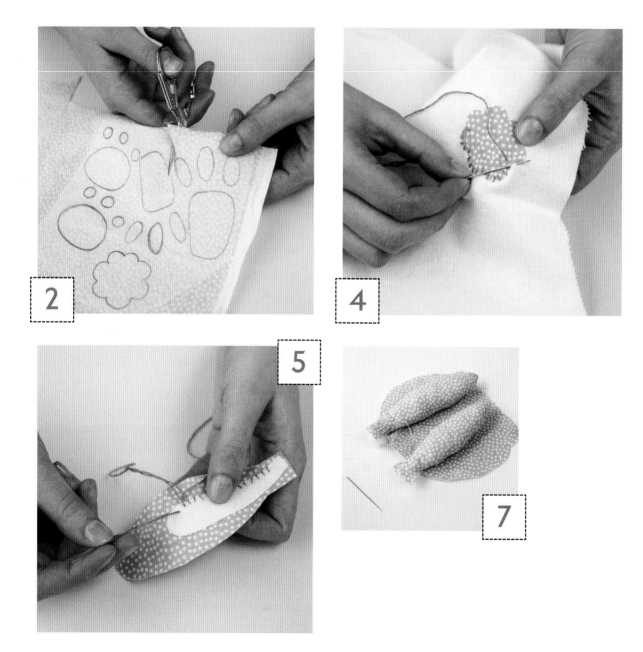

1

Use the templates to make the pattern pieces for the head, ears and blanket body (see pages 106–7). Cut the head and ears from patterned fabric, and the body and inner ears from soft fabric. Use a fabric marker to transfer pattern markings such as the ear positions. The pieces include a seam allowance of 6mm (¼in).

2

Transfer the templates for the front paws, back paws and tail on to the webbing: place the webbing over a template, paper side up, and trace the lines of the template. Cut out the shapes roughly.

3

Place each shape, paper side up, on the wrong side of the patterned fabric. Iron for 3–4 seconds (no steam).

4

Cut out the paws and tail accurately. Peel off the backing paper and lay them, coated side down, on the right side of the body front (paws) and body back (tail). Iron in place and leave to cool (see page 107).

Using three strands of embroidery thread, whipstitch each shape to the body. Make small stitches with a fairly small space between each one. (For details of how to work the hand stitches, see pages 108–11.)

5

Transfer the templates for the inner ears on to the webbing: place the webbing over a template, paper side up, and trace the lines of the template. Cut out the shape roughly.

Place each shape, paper side up, on the wrong side of the soft fabric. Iron for 3–4 seconds (no steam). Cut out the shapes accurately. Peel off the backing paper and lay them, coated side down, on the right side of the front of the ear. Iron in place and leave to cool. Using three

strands of embroidery thread, whipstitch to the ear. Make small stitches with a fairly small space between each one.

6

With the back and front sides of the ear together, right sides facing, machine-stitch all the way around the edges with a 6mm (¼in) seam, leaving the base of the ear open and a gap to turn the pieces inside out.

Turn the ears right side out. Stuff the ears firmly through the gap. You need to make sure there is stuffing right up to the bottom end of each ear, or it will flop rather than stand up. Slipstitch the gap to close it.

7

Lay the front head piece with the right side uppermost. With raw edge to raw edge, position each ear: it should lie on the head with the back of the ear uppermost. Make sure that the tops of the ears extend slightly above the head piece, to ensure that they will be caught securely in the seam. Pin and tack.

instructions

Make the blankie in a neutral colour, or in a traditional pale blue for a boy or pink for a girl. Use a soft fabric such as winceyette or fleece for the body, to make the comforter cosy.

8

Sew the two pieces for the back of the head, right sides together, along the centre back with a 6mm (¼in) seam.

With right sides together, place the front and back head pieces on top of each other. Machine-stitch around the head with a 6mm (¼in) seam, sewing in the ears and leaving the neck edge open. You may find it easier to sew in the ears by hand, using backstitch, because the stuffing may make the head too bulky to go under the machine's foot. Turn the head right side out.

9

If you wish, use an erasable fabric marker or iron-on transfer pen to mark the facial features on the head. Using six strands of black embroidery thread, stitch the nose and mouth using backstitch. Embroider the eyes using satin stitch. Stuff the head firmly. Make sure there is stuffing right up to the bottom end of the neck, or the head will flop rather than standing up.

10

Lay the front of the body with the right side uppermost. Lay the head on top, the back of the head uppermost, with the base of the neck to the edge of the body and the head extending into the body area. Pin and tack.

11

Place the front and back of the body with right sides together, and pin and tack. Machine-stitch all the way around the body, catching in the head, and leaving a gap along the bottom edge for turning. Again, you may find it easier to sew in the head by hand, using backstitch, because the stuffing may make the neck too bulky to go under the machine foot.

Turn the rabbit right side out, pushing out all his paws carefully. Slipstitch the gap to close it. Your little rabbit is ready to be loved!

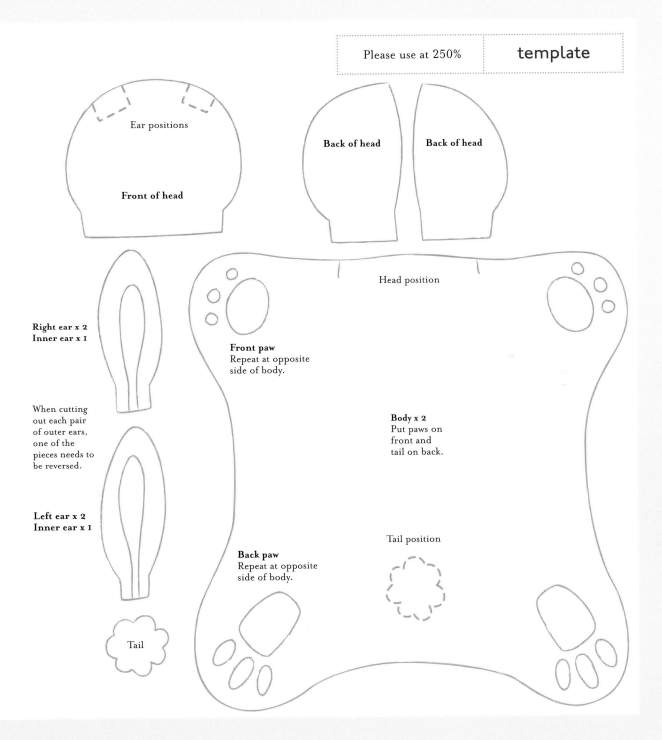

Ear positions

Front of head

Back of head   Back of head

Head position

**Right ear x 2
Inner ear x I**

Front paw
Repeat at opposite
side of body.

When cutting
out each pair
of ears, one of
the pieces needs to
be reversed.

Body x 2
Put paws on
front and
tail on back.

**Left ear x 2
Inner ear x I**

Tail position

Back paw
Repeat at opposite
side of body.

Tail

monster play mat

Little monsters will love playing on this mat: there are plenty of textures and colours to keep them interested. It is also perfect for a baby who is just learning to sit up, or for a slightly older child to lie on and look at a book or take a nap.

instructions

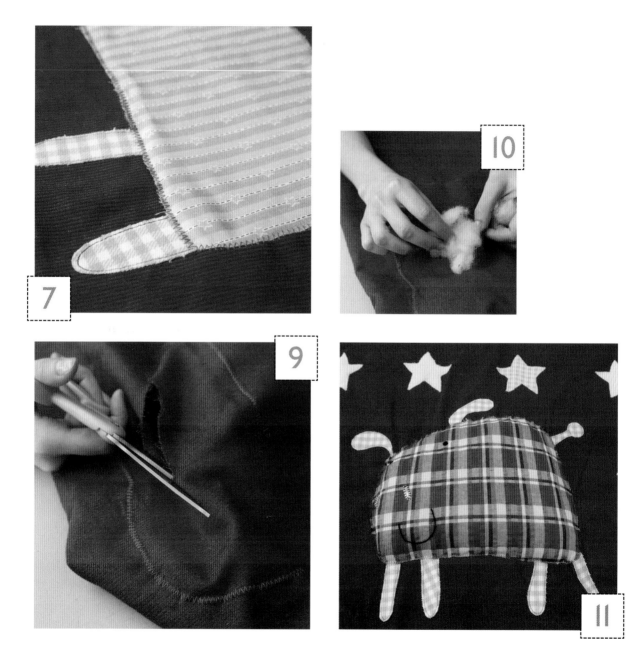

Make the eighteen stars. Transfer the template to the webbing: place the webbing over a template, paper side up, and trace the lines of the template. Cut out the shapes roughly.

Place each shape, paper side up, on the wrong side of the appropriate yellow fabric. Iron for 3–4 seconds (no steam). Cut out the shapes accurately. (Alternatively, iron the webbing on to the back of the fabric and then use a paper template to cut star shapes.)

Cut the fabric for the front surface of the mat: a 1m (1⅛yd) square with a 2cm (¾in) seam allowance all around the edges.

3

Peel off the backing paper from the stars and arrange them, coated side down, to make a border on the right side of the front of the mat – about 10cm (4in) in from the edges. Iron in place and leave to cool (see page 107). Machine-stitch around each motif using zigzag stitch.

4

Make the three monsters. Transfer the templates for the arms, legs, ears, feelers, tail and nostrils to the webbing: place the webbing over a template, paper side up, and trace the lines of the template. Cut out the shapes roughly.

Place each shape, paper side up, on the wrong side of the appropriate fabric. Iron for 3–4 seconds (no steam). Cut out the shapes accurately.

5

Peel off the backing paper from the limbs, tails, ears and feelers and lay them in position, coated side down, on the front of the mat. Remove the backing paper from the nostrils and position on the body of Monster B (not yet attached to the mat) in the same way. Iron everything in place and leave to cool.

Using three strands of embroidery thread, whipstitch each nostril to the body. Make small stitches with a fairly small space between each one. (For details of how to work the hand stitches, see pages 108–11.)

7

Pin the bodies on the front of the mat (ears, feelers, limbs and tail should tuck just under the head/body). Machine-stitch around the edge of the body using zigzag stitch. Machine-stitch around each arm, leg, ear, feeler and tail, just inside the edge, and to outline sections of these, using a straight stitch.

8

Create the monsters' faces. If you wish, use an erasable fabric marker or iron-on transfer pen to mark the facial features on each monster.

instructions

Try to use different textured fabrics, as young children will love to feel the various materials. The mat is in very bright colours, but subtle colours could work just as well.

9

Now stuff the monsters' bodies. Turn the mat front over and cut a small slit in the fabric that lies under each body, being very careful not to cut into the fabric of the body.

10

Ensure that you don't fill the body too full: just add enough stuffing to make the body appear slightly raised.

11

You can now complete the faces. Using six strands of embroidery thread, stitch the mouth using backstitch, and use satin stitch for the eyes.

12

Sew up the slit on the back of each monster with a ladder stitch (make sure the stuffing is evenly spread over the monster). Tie a knot in the thread and bring the needle out to the right side of the fabric. Take the thread horizontally to the other side of the slit, and insert into the fabric. Repeat along the slit, forming what looks like the rungs of a ladder. Finish off.

13

Cut the fabric for the back of the mat to make a 1m (1⅛yd) square with a 2cm (¾in) seam allowance all around the edges. Place the front and back of the mat with right sides together.

14

Machine-stitch around the mat with a 2cm (¾in) seam, leaving a gap for turning along one edge. Turn the right way out.

15

Insert the piece of wadding, making sure it reaches the edges properly and is laid evenly. You may need to trim a tiny bit off the edges to allow it to fit in.

16

Slipstitch the gap in the seam to close it and the mat is ready for a little monster to crawl on!

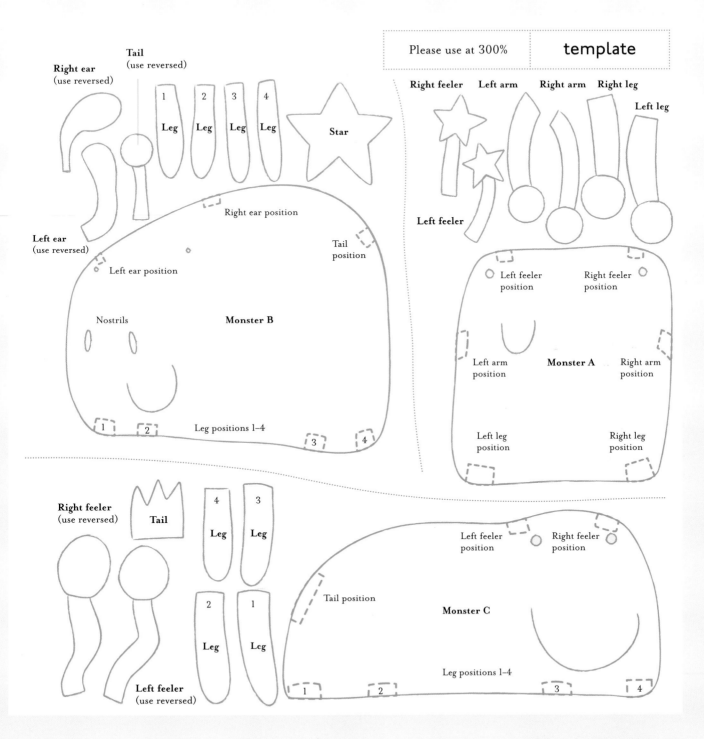

Right ear
(use reversed)

Tail
(use reversed)

1 Leg   2 Leg   3 Leg   4 Leg

Star

Left ear
(use reversed)

Right ear position

Left ear position

Tail position

Nostrils

Monster B

Leg positions 1–4

1   2   3   4

Please use at 300%

template

Right feeler   Left arm   Right arm   Right leg

Left leg

Left feeler

Left feeler position

Right feeler position

Left arm position   Monster A   Right arm position

Left leg position   Right leg position

Right feeler
(use reversed)

Tail

4 Leg   3 Leg

2 Leg   1 Leg

Left feeler
(use reversed)

Left feeler position   Right feeler position

Tail position

Monster C

Leg positions 1–4

1   2   3   4

doggy draught excluder

You will need

Patterned cotton fabric: 1m
(1^{1}/$_{8}$yd) (body)

Scraps of contrasting cotton
fabric (ears, legs and tail)

Scrap of brown cotton fabric
(nose)

Double-sided fusible webbing
(such as Bondaweb) (nose)

Embroidery thread (black)

Embroidery needle

Sewing machine

Sewing thread

Toy stuffing

Gravel or dried beans
(optional)

This friendly dog will sit happily in front of the door, keeping out draughts, and you'll never have to tell him to 'Stay'. If you like, you can add some weight to his body and use him as a doorstop as well. Make him in colours to match the theme of the nursery.

instructions

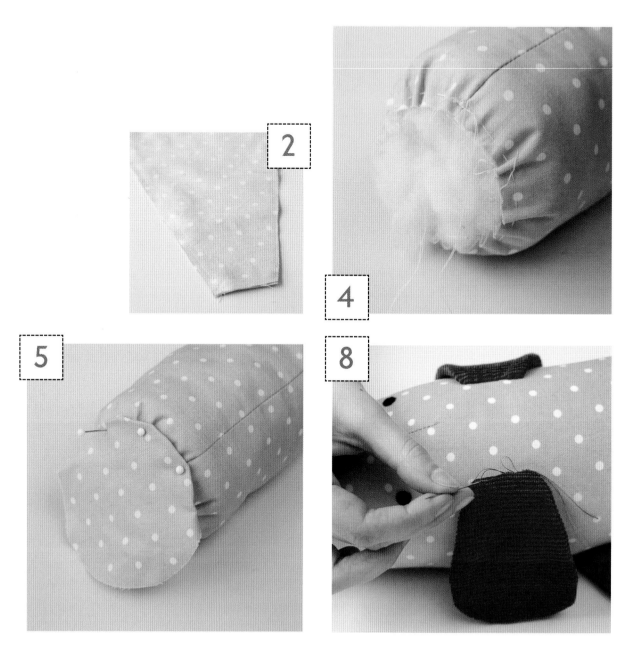

Use the templates to make pattern pieces and cut out the rear end circle, ears, legs, and tail (see page 106) in the appropriate fabrics. For the body, extend the length of the template until it measures about 23½in (60cm). The pieces should include a seam allowance of 6mm (¼in).

Fold the body piece in half, with right sides together, matching the letters (A with A and B with B). Pin and tack. Machine-stitch along the underside of the body/head (the long edge) and the angled edge of the top of the head, but leave the nose and tail ends open.

3

Run a gathering thread (by hand) around the nose end, then draw up the stitches to close the gap and secure with a few stitches. (For details of how to work the hand stitches, see pages 108–11.)

Turn the body the right way out and stuff firmly with toy stuffing. If you want to add some weight, you can put gravel or dried beans in the base of the body. If you do this – especially with gravel – I recommend that you use a double thickness of fabric for the body.

Run a gathering stitch right around the dog's rear end. (Sew by hand or use a large stitch on the machine.) Pull up the threads slightly, but do not tighten too much.

5

Pin the rear end circle over the dog's rear end. Turning in a 6mm (¼in) hem as you go, whipstitch the circle to the body.

6

Transfer the nose template to the webbing: place the webbing over the template, paper side up, and trace the lines of the template. Cut out the shape roughly. Place the shape, paper side up, on the wrong side of the brown fabric. Iron for 3–4 seconds (no steam). Cut out the shape accurately.

7

Peel off the backing paper and position the nose, coated side down, on the narrow end and pin. (The top of the dog is the side with the small seam rather than the seam that goes all the way to the tail end.)

Sew on the nose using three strands of embroidery thread and whipstitch (make small stitches with a fairly small space between each one). Secure the thread to the body under the nose to start, and finish the stitching just under the edge of the nose. To hide the end of the thread, push the needle into the body and bring it out some distance away, so the thread is lost within the body.

Make the ears. Place the pieces with right sides together and machine-stitch around the edges with a 6mm (¼in) seam

instructions

Add dried beans or gravel to make him heavier, but sew in a lining if you use gravel.

allowance, leaving a gap in the straight side for turning. Turn right side out. Turn the open edges to the inside and slipstitch to close.

Position the ears on the dog, using the photo for guidance, and sew on firmly. Use a double thickness of thread and whipstitch. Secure the thread to the body under the ears to start, and finish the stitching under the ear, close to the top, so the stitches will be hidden.

Make the tail and legs. Place the pieces with right sides together and machine-stitch around the edges with a 6mm ($^{1}/_{4}$in) seam, leaving the end that attaches to the body open. Turn right side out and stuff quite firmly.

Whipstitch the legs to the body, turning in 6mm ($^{1}/_{4}$in) at the top of the leg. Sew right around the edges, forming a circle. Secure the thread to the body under the leg to start, and finish

the stitching just under the top of the leg. Repeat the procedure to attach the tail.

Embroider the facial features. Use backstitch for a smiling mouth and satin stitch for the eyes. Sew an eye, go down to the mouth with the same piece of thread and then go back to do the other eye.

12

This little sausage dog is now ready to guard the nursery door, keeping draughts out and the heat in.

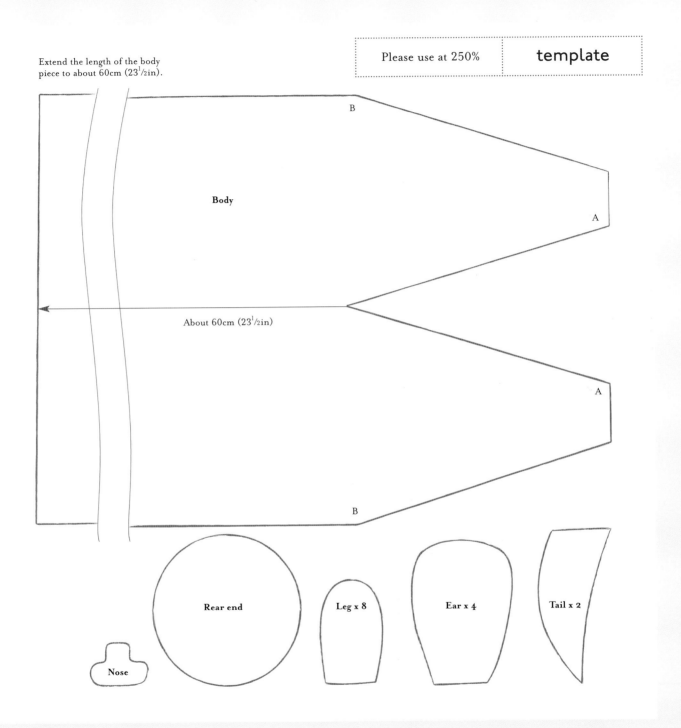

Extend the length of the body piece to about 60cm (23$\frac{1}{2}$in).

B

A

Body

About 60cm (23$\frac{1}{2}$in)

A

B

Nose

Rear end

Leg x 8

Ear x 4

Tail x 2

kitten cushion

You will need

Striped fabric: 0.5m x 114cm
($\frac{1}{2}$yd x 45in) (cushion front)

Patterned cotton, corduroy, or
brushed cotton winceyette:
0.5m x 114cm ($\frac{1}{2}$yd x 45in)
(cushion back)

Scraps of cream corduroy
fabric (circles and part-
circles)

Scraps of three different
patterned cotton fabrics
(kittens)

Double-sided fusible webbing
(such as Bondaweb) (circles,
part-circles and kittens)

Embroidery thread (black,
green, blue, pink, beige,
or colours to suit)

Embroidery needle

Sewing machine with
a freehand foot

Sewing thread

Ruler and set square

Iron-on transfer pen

Cushion pad: 40 x 40cm
(16 x 16in)

All little children love kittens, and the three that live on this cute cushion are very appealing. The design features cord circles to give added texture, but fleece would work equally well. For a boy's room, choose a suitable colour scheme.

instructions

Cut a 43 x 43cm (17 x 17in) square of striped fabric.

Place the webbing, paper side up, on the wrong side of the corduroy. Iron for 3–4 seconds (no steam). Use the templates to cut out the circles and circle sections (see page 106–7).

2

Peel off the backing paper and lay the shapes, coated side down, on the right side of the striped fabric – the corner circle sections should align with the edges. Iron in place and leave to cool (see page 107).

3

Transfer the kitten template to the webbing to make three kittens: place the webbing over the template, paper side up, and trace it. Cut out the shapes roughly. Place each shape, paper side up, on the wrong side of the appropriate fabric. Iron for 3–4 seconds (no steam). Cut out the shapes accurately.

4

Peel off the backing paper and lay the kittens, coated side down, on the front of the cushion. Iron in place and leave to cool.

Using the freehand foot, machine-stitch carefully around each piece just inside the edge, using a thread in a contrasting colour. You can use an embroidery hoop if you wish.

5

Transfer the kittens' facial features to greaseproof paper, using an iron-on transfer pen (see page 107). Iron on to the kitten so the eyes, inner ears, whiskers, nose and mouth are all in the right position.

6

Sew on the facial features using three strands of embroidery thread: use backstitch for the mouth and whiskers, and satin stitch for the other features. (For details of how to work the hand stitches, see pages 108–11.)

Using three strands of embroidery thread, sew around each circle using whipstitch. Make small stitches with a fairly small space between each one.

Make the back of the cushion. Cut two rectangles of the soft fabric, measuring 43 x 28cm (17 x 11in). On each piece, fold over 4cm (1½in) on the long edge to the wrong side, tuck the raw edge under and hem.

8

Place the back and front of the cushion with right sides together, with the hemmed edges of the back facing towards the centre of the cushion (these pieces overlap). Pin around all four edges, tack and then machine-stitch with a 1.5cm (½in) seam. Reinforce the corners by stitching over them again with a small stitch. Trim the seam and trim diagonally across the corners.

Turn the cushion cover the right side out. Slip the cushion pad through the back opening.

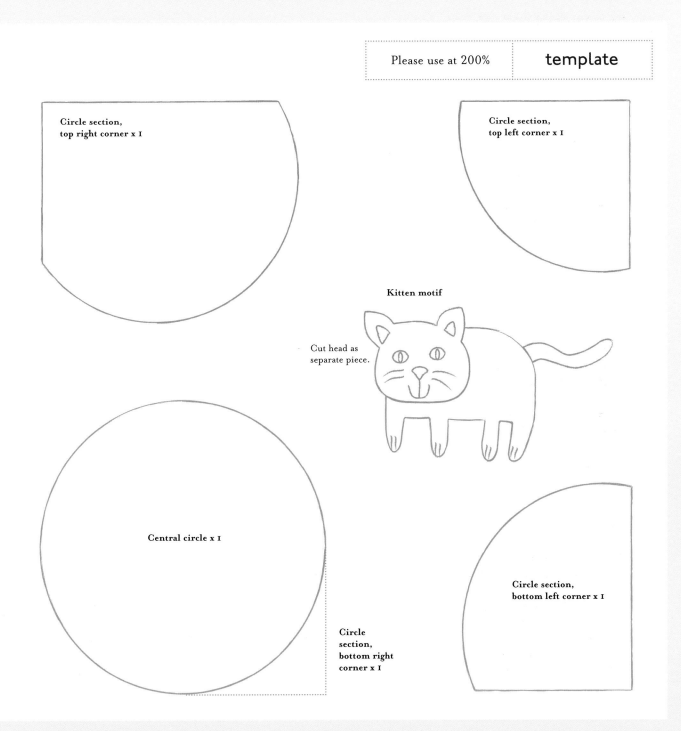

Circle section,
top right corner x 1

Circle section,
top left corner x 1

Kitten motif

Cut head as
separate piece.

Central circle x 1

Circle
section,
bottom right
corner x 1

Circle section,
bottom left corner x 1

animal textile picture

You will need

Corduroy fabric: a little bigger than the picture frame (background)

Scraps of patterned cotton fabrics (animals, food and decorative line)

Double-sided fusible webbing (such as Bondaweb) (animals)

Embroidery thread (black, blue and orange, or colours to suit)

Embroidery needle

Sewing machine with a freehand foot

Sewing thread

Erasable fabric marker

Ruler and set square

Picture frame: about 25 x 20cm (10 x 8in)

This picture is very simple to make, and you can reduce or enlarge the pattern pieces for a different sized frame. It mainly features machine stitch, but you could work stitches by hand to add more texture and depth.

instructions

Transfer the templates for the mouse, cat, dog, cheese, fish and bone to the webbing: place the webbing over the template, paper side up, and trace the lines of the template. Cut out the shape roughly. Place each shape, paper side up, on the wrong side of the appropriate fabric. Iron for 3–4 seconds (no steam). Cut out the shapes accurately.

Tack a rectangle on the corduroy to mark out the dimensions of the image area that will be displayed in the picture frame. Do this by cutting a rectangle of paper and sewing around it, or draw the shape on the cloth with an erasable fabric marker.

Peel off the backing paper and lay the motifs, coated side down, on the front of the corduroy background, using the photo for guidance on positioning. Iron in place and leave to cool (see page 107).

Using the freehand foot, machine-stitch carefully around each motif just inside the edge, and to highlight details as shown in the photo. Sew a few stitches at the bottom of the dog's legs to represent claws. You can use an embroidery hoop if you wish.

5

Use black embroidery thread for facial features: make French knots for the eyes, use satin stitch for the noses, and backstitch for the mouths and whiskers. (For details of how to work the hand stitches, see pages 108–11.)

6

Embroider decorative dividing lines between the animals. Create a line of cross-stitch under the mouse. Use the fabric marker to mark a line of dots, 1cm (3/8in) apart, beginning at the edge. Using six strands of embroidery thread, sew a cross over each dot, to make a row of cross-stitch with a small gap between each cross.

7

Create another decorative line under the cat with a narrow strip of appliquéd fabric plus a line of running stitch. Use the template to cut out the strip of fabric, then pin and tack it under the cat. Machine-stitch along it with two intersecting wavy lines. Using six strands of embroidery thread, sew a line of running stitch under the appliquéd strip.

8

Trim around the tacked rectangle, leaving a border of about 3cm (1¼in) to hold the picture in the frame.

9

Frame the picture and display it in the nursery.

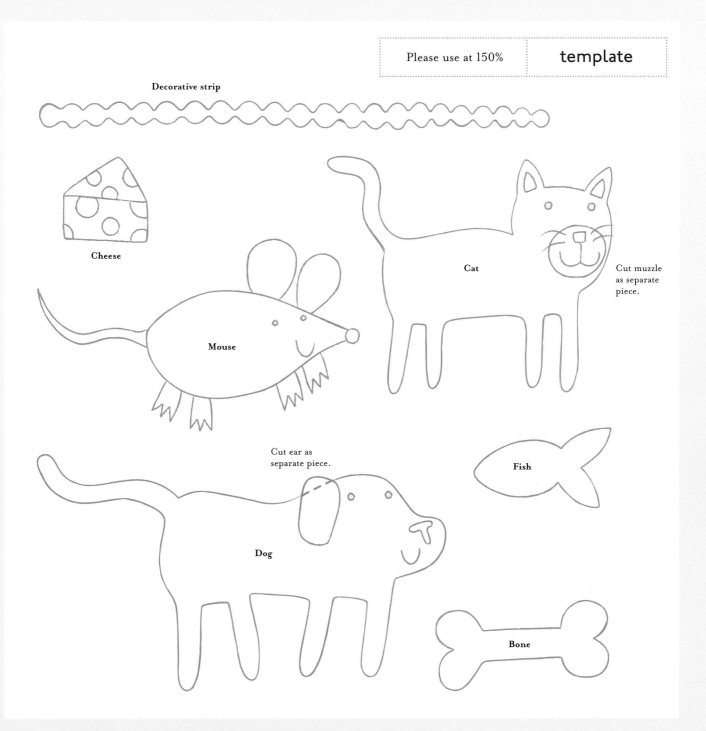

Decorative strip

Cheese

Mouse

Cat

Cut muzzle as separate piece.

Cut ear as separate piece.

Dog

Fish

Bone

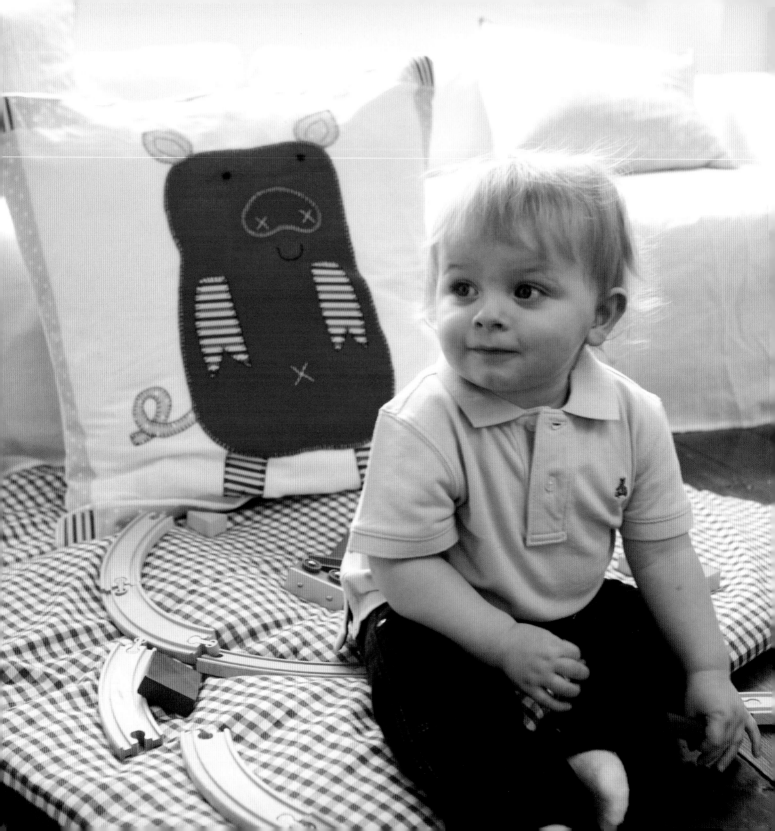

giant piggy cushion

This cushion matches Henry the Pig on page 62: you may like to make them both in matching fabrics. It would make a delightful decorative cushion for a bed or a rocking chair in a nursery, a fun seat for a book corner, or a squashy place for a baby to lie.

instructions

1

Cut a square of soft fabric for the cushion front, 69 x 69cm (27 x 27in).

Make the borders and corner squares. Cut the webbing: four rectangles, 69 x 6.5cm (27 x 2½in), and four squares, 6.5 x 6.5cm (2½ x 2½in). Fix the webbing to the fabric: place it, paper side up, on the wrong side of the fabric. Iron for 3–4 seconds (no steam).

Cut out the shapes, peel off the backing paper and lay them, coated side down, on the right side of the front of the cushion. Iron in place and leave to cool (see pages 106–7).

Machine-stitch around the edges of the corner square/border pieces using a zigzag stitch (not the outer edge: it will be caught in the cushion's seam).

2

Make the pig. Transfer the templates to the webbing: place the webbing over the template, paper side up, and trace the lines of the template. Cut out the shape roughly. Place each shape, paper side up, on the wrong side of the appropriate fabric. Iron for 3–4 seconds (no steam). Cut out the shapes accurately.

Peel off the backing paper and lay the pieces, coated side down, on the front of the cushion. Tuck the ends of the back legs, ears and tail behind the main body piece. Iron in place and leave to cool.

Sew blanket stitch around the edge of each piece, using six strands of embroidery thread. (For details of how to work the hand stitches, see pages 108–11.)

Sew on the facial features, using six strands of black embroidery thread. Use satin stitch for the eyes and backstitch for the mouth. If you prefer to have a drawn line to follow, use an erasable fabric marker or iron-on transfer pen (see page 107).

Using six strands of embroidery thread, backstitch a cross for a tummy button and two crosses for nostrils.

Make the back of the cushion. Cut two rectangles of the soft fabric, measuring 69 x 42cm (27 x 16½in). On each piece, fold over 4cm (1½in) on the long edge to the wrong side, tuck the raw edge under and hem.

6

Place the back and front of the cushion with right sides together, with the hemmed edges of the back facing towards the centre of the cushion (these pieces overlap). Pin around all four edges, tack and then sew with a 1.5cm (½in) seam. Reinforce the corners by stitching over them again with a small stitch. Trim the seam and trim across the corners.

7

Turn the cushion cover the right side out, then slip the cushion pad through the back opening.

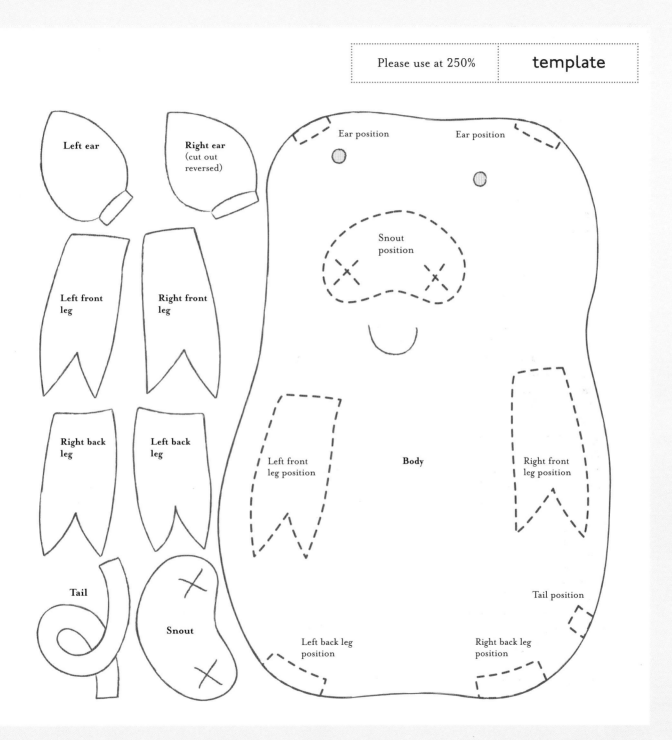

Left ear

Right ear
(cut out reversed)

Left front leg

Right front leg

Right back leg

Left back leg

Tail

Snout

Ear position   Ear position

Snout position

Left front leg position

Body

Right front leg position

Left back leg position

Right back leg position

Tail position

henry the pig

Corduroy fabric in a bright colour: 0.25m x 114cm ($^1/_4$yd x 45in) (body and snout)

Scraps of striped cotton fabric (legs)

Scraps of patterned cotton fabric (ears and tail)

Double-sided fusible webbing (such as Bondaweb) (tail)

Embroidery thread (black, red and blue, or colours to suit)

Embroidery needle

Sewing machine

Sewing thread

Erasable fabric marker or iron-on transfer pen

Toy stuffing

Henry is a charming pig: he is loyal, friendly and very cute! He is very huggable, too, and his corduroy body gives him an interesting texture. You could make a pair of porkers – change Henry into Henrietta by using a paler corduroy and a more subtle striped material for the limbs.

instructions

Use the templates to cut out the pattern pieces (see page 106): the body pieces in corduroy, the legs in striped fabric and the ears and tail in patterned fabric. Use a fabric marker to transfer pattern markings such as the ear positions (see page 107.)

Make the ears. Backstitch the line of the inner ear on the front ear piece using six strands of embroidery thread. (For details of how to work the hand stitches, see pages 108–11.) Place the front and back of the ear with wrong sides together. Sew around the edge in blanket stitch, leaving the bottom open. Stuff the ears (you need to make sure there is stuffing right up to the bottom end of each ear, or it will flop rather than stand up).

Make the legs. Place the two back pieces with right sides together and machine-stitch along the back of the leg (the long, slightly curved edge) with a 6mm (¼in) seam.

Take the front leg piece and place it on the back piece, right sides together. Sew around the edge with a 6mm (¼in) seam, leaving the top of the leg open. Turn right side out, using a pencil to gently push out the points. Stuff firmly.

Transfer the template for the tail to the webbing: place the webbing over the template, paper side up, and trace the lines of the template. Cut out the shape roughly. Place the shape, paper side up, on the wrong side of the fabric. Iron for 3–4 seconds (no steam).

Cut out the shape accurately. Peel off the backing paper and lay it, coated side down, on the wrong side of the fabric. Iron in place and leave to cool (see page 107). Cut out the double-sided tail. Sew around the shape with blanket stitch, as for the ears.

Attach the legs and ears to the front body piece. Lay them on the right side of the body in the marked positions, with raw edges together and the limbs and ears lying on the body (the back of each is uppermost, so everything faces the correct way when the pig is finished). Pin and tack in place. Make sure that the tops of the ears and limbs extend slightly above the body piece, so they will be caught securely in the seam.

7

Make up the back body piece: place the two sections with right sides together and machine-stitch along the pig's backbone with a 6mm (¼in) seam.

8

Take the gusset piece for the pig's rear end and pin at the bottom of the front body, with right sides together, so the centre lies in the middle of the space between his legs. Tack.

instructions

The snout is a little tricky: remember to make the whipstitches close together when you attach it to the body, so the stuffing doesn't poke out.

9

Place the back and front body with right sides together, then pin round as far as the gusset and tack. Machine-stitch around the body as far as each side of the gusset with a 6mm (¼in) seam. Continue stitching from the top of the gusset around the front body piece, trapping in the legs. Sew around the back gusset, leaving a gap in the middle for turning.

10

Turn the pig right side out. Sew a cross for a tummy button, using six strands of embroidery thread. Stuff the body.

11

Make the snout. Take the long strip and fold with right sides together. Machine-stitch the narrow end with a 6mm (¼in) seam. Press the seam open with your fingers. With right sides together, pin on the front of the snout, with the dip in the snout over the join. Tack all the way round, making sure it all matches well, then machine-stitch with a 6mm (¼in) seam. (If you prefer, you can sew the snout together by hand.)

12

Stuff the snout lightly. Embroider on two crosses with six strands of embroidery thread for the nostrils. Position the snout on the face. Slipstitch around the edge to attach it,

turning under 6mm (¼in). Before you complete the sewing, stuff the snout more firmly.

13

Embroider the facial features using three strands of black embroidery thread. For the eyes, backstitch a small circle and then fill it with satin stitch. Sew two layers to make the eyes slightly raised. Backstitch the mouth using the photo to guide you.

14

Slipstitch the gap in the pig's rear end to close it (when you reach the middle of the gap, tuck in the tip of the tail and sew it into position).

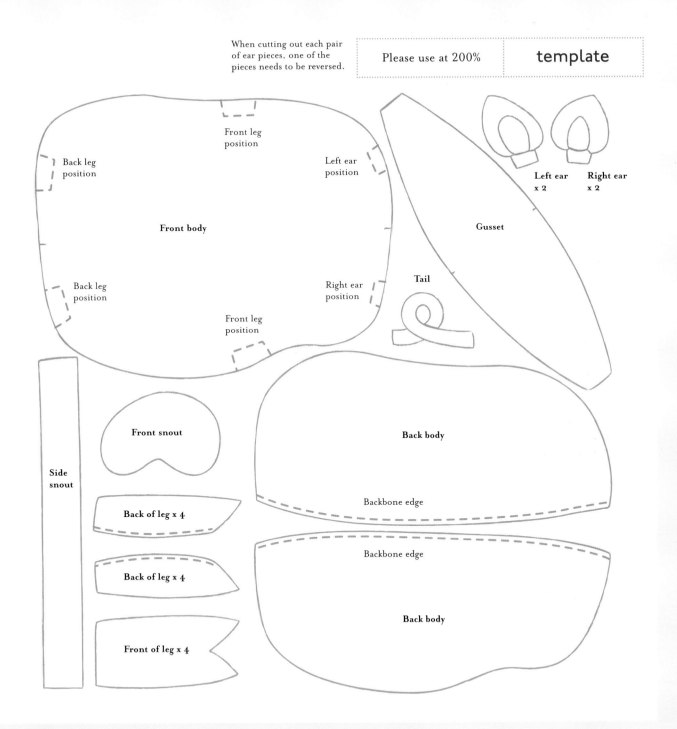

When cutting out each pair of ear pieces, one of the pieces needs to be reversed.

Please use at 200%

template

Back leg position

Front leg position

Left ear position

Front body

Gusset

Left ear x 2

Right ear x 2

Back leg position

Right ear position

Tail

Front leg position

Side snout

Front snout

Back body

Back of leg x 4

Backbone edge

Back of leg x 4

Backbone edge

Front of leg x 4

Back body

sleepy ted mobile

The sleepy teddies and moon and stars dangling from this mobile contain a lot of small stitches and intricate detail, so if you love sewing, it will be perfect for you. The mobile is bound to become a treasured keepsake.

You will need

Hoop: about 20cm (8in) in diameter

Strip of patterned cotton fabric: approx. 130 x 5cm (51 x 2in) (hoop)

Scraps of patterned cotton fabrics (teddies and hats)

Scraps of corduroy (tummy and inner ears)

Scraps of yellow patterned cotton fabrics (moon and stars)

Double-sided fusible webbing (such as Bondaweb) (teddies, moon and stars)

Embroidery thread (black and various colours)

Embroidery needle

Ribbon: two pieces, different colours, each approx. 3m x 4mm ($3\frac{1}{3}$yd x $\frac{1}{4}$in)

Erasable fabric marker or iron-on transfer pen (optional)

Toy stuffing

instructions

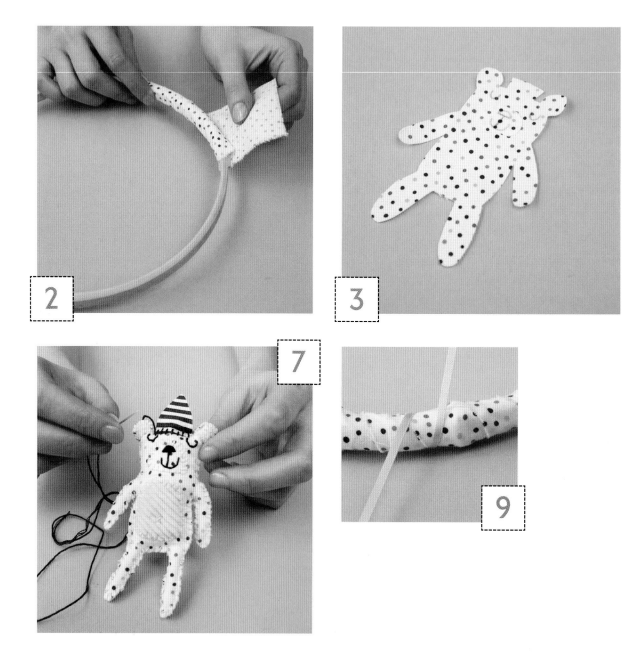

1

Transfer the templates for making the three teddies, moon and three stars to the webbing: place the webbing over the template, paper side up, and trace the lines. Cut out the shape roughly then place, paper side up, on the wrong side of the relevant fabric. Iron for 3–4 seconds (no steam). Cut out the shapes accurately. Peel off the backing paper but leave on the teddy pieces.

2

Take the strip of fabric for the hoop (for a frayed-edge look, tear the fabric rather than cut it). Wind it tightly around the hoop (you can use separate pieces if you wish and just make sure the ends are tucked in tightly). Sew a small stitch at the end to prevent it unravelling.

3

Lay the inner ears, muzzle and tummy, coated side down, on the front of the bear. Iron in place and leave to cool (see page 107).

You can now remove the paper.

Using three strands of black embroidery thread, sew on the teddies' facial features. If you prefer to have a drawn line to follow, use an erasable fabric marker or iron-on transfer pen (see page 107). Use satin stitch for the nose and backstitch for the mouth. For eyes that are open, make French knots; for eyes that are closed, use backstitch. (For details of how to work the hand stitches, see pages 108–11.)

4

Whipstitch around the tummy, muzzle and inner ears using three strands of embroidery thread (make small stitches with a fairly small space between each one). Add a cross to the tummy centre to make a tummy button.

5

Place the front and back of each teddy with wrong sides together; pin and tack. Whipstitch the sections together along the edges with three strands of embroidery thread (leave the tab at the top open). Stuff lightly.

6

Cut seven pieces of ribbon for suspending the teddies, stars and moon (see steps 9 and 10), making the ribbon for the moon longer than the others. Trim once tied to the hoop.

7

Take a teddy and a length of ribbon and tuck it into the gap in the teddy's head.

Then take one side of the hat and sew it to the tab, wrong side of the hat to right side of the tab, catching in the ribbon. Use three strands of embroidery thread and whipstitch. Repeat with the other half of the hat.

Whipstitch the hat all the way around the edges, making sure the ribbon is hanging straight.

8

Repeat for the other teddies. Make the stars and moon in the same way, embroidering the face before joining the sections. Make French knots for the eyes and backstitch the nose and mouth.

instructions

If you have a specific nursery theme, make a mobile to match, using the techniques for this project.

9

Take one teddy and ribbon and wrap the ribbon around the hoop, as in the photo, making sure the teddy will face outwards. Secure the ribbon to the hoop with a little stitch just inside the rim, leaving a long tail for tying with all the other ribbons above the hoop.

Do this with the other teddies and stars, alternating them at equal intervals around the edge, each hanging at a slightly different depth.

10

Hold the mobile by the ribbons and make sure it hangs straight. Add the moon's ribbon to the bundle, then knot all the ribbons together. You may need to adjust it so that the ring is level. Tie the loose ends into a bow or another knot, so the mobile can be suspended from a hook. The mobile is now ready to hang in the nursery – perfect for helping a little person to get to sleep!

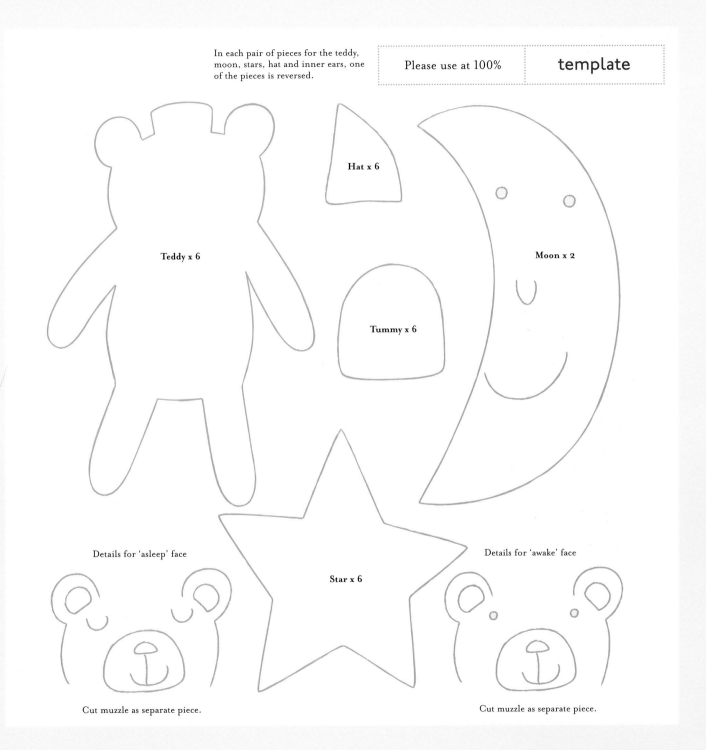

In each pair of pieces for the teddy, moon, stars, hat and inner ears, one of the pieces is reversed.

Please use at 100%

template

Hat x 6

Teddy x 6

Moon x 2

Tummy x 6

Details for 'asleep' face

Star x 6

Details for 'awake' face

Cut muzzle as separate piece.

Cut muzzle as separate piece.

toy tidy

A toy tidy will encourage toddlers to put away their toys without too much fuss! The cord pockets are durable, so lots of things can be stuffed inside. Hang this tidy from a dado rail, or set two small hooks in the perfect place on the wall.

instructions

6

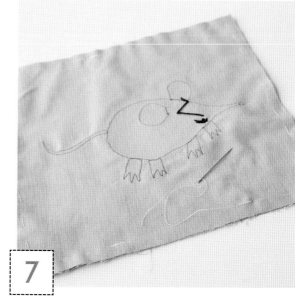

7

10

If you want a bigger tidy, make the main pieces bigger and add more pockets, repeating the animals.

Cut the front and back from striped fabric, with the stripes running vertically. Make each piece 83 x 63cm (33 x 25in).

Cut the pieces for the six pockets out of the corduroy: you need twelve rectangles, 23 x 25cm (9 x 10in).

Make the animals. Transfer the templates to the webbing: place the webbing over a template, paper side up, and trace the lines of the template. Cut out the shapes roughly. Place each shape, paper side up, on the wrong side of the appropriate fabric. For the sheep's head and legs, and the rabbit's and cat's inner ears, use a fabric that contrasts with the body. Iron for 3–4 seconds (no steam). Cut out the shapes accurately.

Peel off the backing paper from the animals and arrange the bodies, coated side down, on the right side of six of the pocket pieces (long sides are top and bottom). Iron in place and leave to cool (see page 107). Attach other parts such as the sheep's face and legs (tuck under the body), and details such as inner ears, in the same way.

Using the freehand foot, machine-stitch around each animal, just inside the edge, using a straight stitch. Repeat to highlight other features on the animals, as shown in the photos. A thread in a contrasting colour looks good. You can hand-stitch these pieces if you prefer.

Create the animals' faces. If you wish, use an erasable fabric marker or iron-on transfer pen to mark the facial features on each creature.

Using six strands of black embroidery thread, stitch the mouths using backstitch, make French knots for the eyes (satin stitch for the eyes on the rabbit and pig), and satin stitch for the noses on the dog and cat. For nostrils, use cross-stitch on the pig and backstitch on the sheep. (For details of how to work the hand stitches, see pages 108–11.)

Place the back and front of each pocket with right sides together, and pin and tack. Machine-stitch around the edges with a 1.5cm (½in) seam, leaving a small gap along the bottom for turning right side out.

instructions

If your child has a favourite animal, use that as inspiration for a single motif, repeated in different colours and patterns.

8

Turn all the pockets right side out and press. Slipstitch the edges of the gaps to close them.

Position the pockets on the striped front piece, roughly 6.5cm (2½in) from all the edges (includes a 1.5cm/½in seam allowance for attaching the front piece to the back). Make sure that the pockets are straight, with a gap of 5cm (2in) between each pocket on each edge.

9

Pin and tack the pockets. Machine-stitch around the sides and bottom, leaving the top open, using zigzag stitch in a colour taken from the animal on the pocket.

10

Now make the hangers for the top of the tidy. Cut two rectangles of striped fabric, 27 x 9cm (10½ x 3½in). Fold in half lengthways, with right sides together, and sew along the long edge with a 1.5cm (½in) seam. Turn inside out and press.

Referring to the photo, fold each piece into a handle with a straight top. Insert pins to hold the shape.

11

Place the hangers on the front of the tidy, with raw edges together and the hanger lying against the front of the tidy, and roughly lining up the outer edges with the outer edge of the pockets. Pin and tack.

12

Take the back piece of the tidy and pin it to the front, right sides together. Sew right around the edges with a 1.5cm (½in) seam, leaving a gap along the bottom edge that is big enough for turning the tidy.

13

Turn the tidy right side out, pushing out each edge fully. Press the edges. Slipstitch the gap to close it and the tidy is ready to store favourite toys.

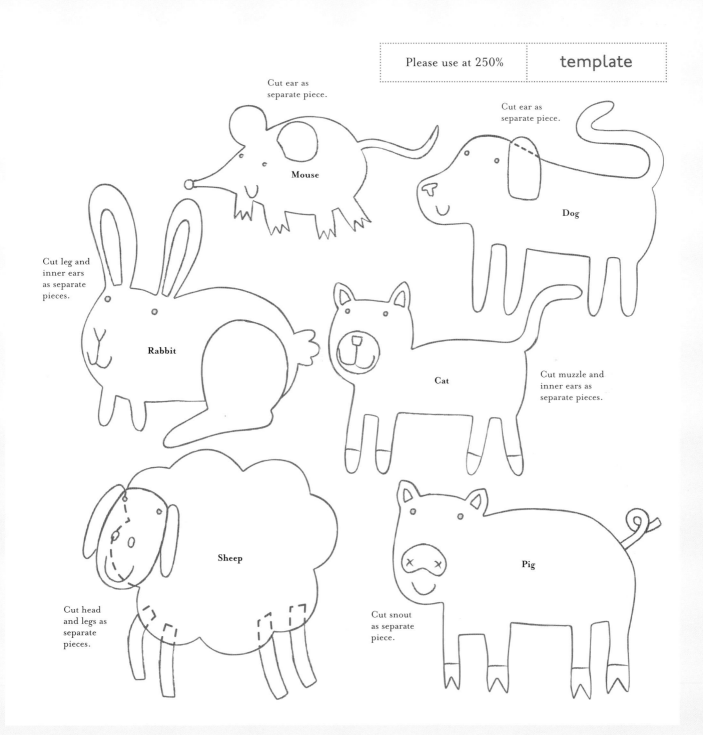

Cut ear as separate piece.

Mouse

Cut ear as separate piece.

Dog

Cut leg and inner ears as separate pieces.

Rabbit

Cat

Cut muzzle and inner ears as separate pieces.

Sheep

Cut head and legs as separate pieces.

Pig

Cut snout as separate piece.

Please use at 250%   template

ella the mouse

Ella is quite a shy mouse, but she will be a good friend to any little person who loves her. Ella has lovely beady eyes; if you are making her for an older child, you could use real beads, but make sure you sew them on very securely.

instructions

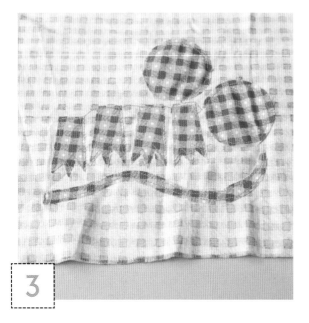

3

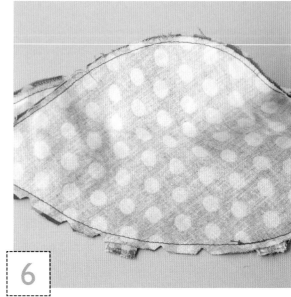

6

7

For an older child, you could add dried beans to the mouse to give it more weight.

Use the templates to cut out the pattern pieces for the body and ears. Use a fabric marker to transfer pattern markings such as ear positions (see pages 106–7).

Make the legs, nose and tail. Transfer the templates to the webbing: place the webbing over the template, paper side up, and trace the lines. Cut out the shape roughly, leaving a border. Place the shape, paper side up, on the wrong side of the fabric. Iron for 3–4 seconds (no steam). Cut out the pieces, then peel off the backing paper.

Lay the legs and tail, coated side down, on the wrong side of the fabric (choose a piece that is big enough to fit into an embroidery hoop, and that can accommodate the ears as well as the legs and tail). Iron the legs and tail in place to make double-sided items, and leave to cool (see page 107).

Cut out the ears and tack these to the same piece of fabric as the legs, wrong sides together. Now the legs, tail and ears are ready to sew. Put the piece of fabric into an embroidery hoop and machine-stitch around the legs, ears and tail just inside the edges (or stitch by hand), as you can see in the picture. Leave the straight edge of the ear open – this is going to be stuffed so it doesn't need to be bonded down.

Carefully cut out all of the pieces. The ears are constructed so that they will end up with a slightly frayed edge.

Make up the body (there are two sections for the side body and one section for the underside).

For the side body: position the tail on the right side of one section where marked, with raw edges together and the tail lying on the body. Pin the two side body sections with right sides together, then tack. Machine-stitch with a 6mm ($\frac{1}{4}$in) seam along the backbone, sewing in the tail as you go.

Lay the legs on the right side of the side body pieces where marked, with raw edges together. Make sure that the tops of the legs extend slightly above the body piece, to ensure that they will be caught securely in the seam. Pin and tack in place.

6

With right sides together, join the upper body to the underside. Machine-stitch around the body with a 6mm ($\frac{1}{4}$in) seam, leaving a gap at the rear end for turning. Cut triangular notches out of the seam allowance to reduce bulk, so that when the mouse is turned right side out, the seam is smooth and not bumpy.

7

Turn the mouse the right way out and stuff quite firmly. If she is for an older child, you can always add dried beans to give her more weight.

instructions

Make a mouse-shaped cushion by enlarging the pattern pieces on a photocopier.

8

Whipstitch the nose in place, using three strands of embroidery thread. (For details of how to work the hand stitches, see pages 108–11.)

Stuff the ears lightly and whipstitch them neatly and securely to the body using three strands of embroidery thread.

9

Embroider facial features using six strands of black embroidery thread. For the eyes, backstitch a small circle and then fill it with satin stitch. Sew two layers to make the eyes slightly raised. Backstitch the mouth.

10

Add a little more stuffing, then sew up the gap in the mouse's rear end using slipstitch. This can be a bit fiddly, as you have to fold the seam in as you go. Fold in enough for the underside to meet the other sides of the mouse smoothly.

In each pair of pieces for the side body, legs, ears and tail, one of the pieces is reversed (legs and tail are double-sided items).

Please use at 200%

template

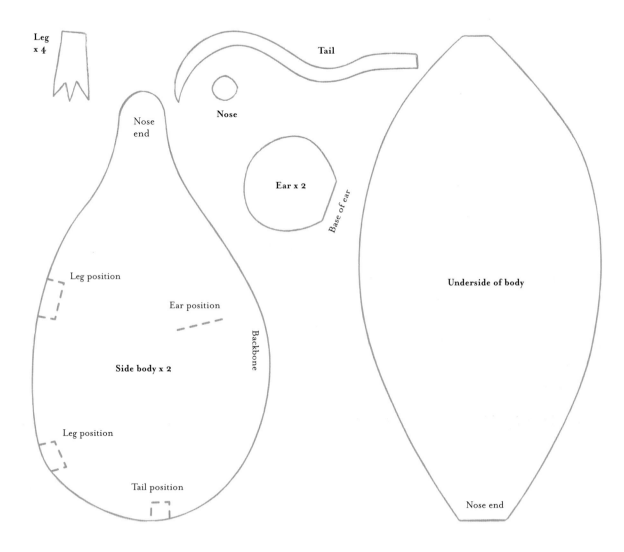

Leg x 4

Tail

Nose

Nose end

Ear x 2

Base of ear

Underside of body

Leg position

Ear position

Backbone

Side body x 2

Leg position

Tail position

Nose end

olivia the sheep

You will need

White or cream fleece:
41 x 22cm (16 x 8½in) (body)

Scraps of pale patterned
cotton fabric (head, ears, tail
and legs)

Embroidery thread (black and
yellow, or colour to suit)

Embroidery needle

Sewing machine

Sewing thread

Toy stuffing

Olivia is a lively sheep and can't wait to get up to mischief with her new owner! She is bound to be a hit: her soft, round body is very cuddly and her little legs give her a slightly comic appearance.

instructions

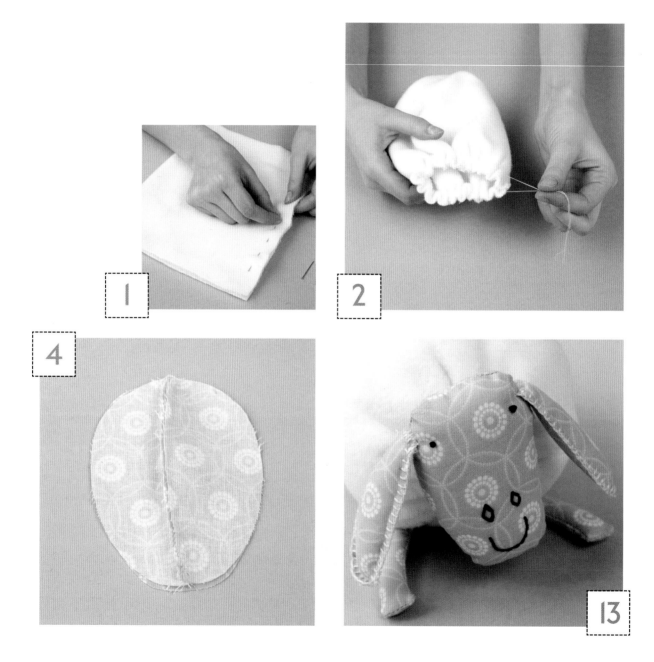

1

Make the sheep's body. Fold the rectangle of fleece in half widthways, with right sides together, so the two shorter sides meet. Pin and tack along the short edge. Machine-stitch with a 1.5cm ($\frac{1}{2}$in) seam, leaving a gap in the middle for turning.

2

Run a gathering stitch all the way around one of the ends, 6mm ($\frac{1}{4}$in) away from the edge, and pull it up tightly. The body now looks something like a cracker. Sew over and over the end so that no hole remains, flattening the sticking-out bit as you do so. Repeat at the other end of the body.

3

Turn the body right side out and stuff quite firmly.

4

Use the templates to cut out the pieces for the head (see pages 106–7). Place the two pieces for the back of the head with right sides together. Pin, tack and machine-stitch with a 6mm ($\frac{1}{4}$in) seam.

Pin the front and back of the head with right sides together, then tack. Machine-stitch around the edge with a 6mm ($\frac{1}{4}$in) seam, leaving a gap for turning. Turn right side out and stuff.

5

Use the templates to cut out the pieces for the ears (see pages 106–7). Place the two pieces for each ear with wrong sides together. Pin and tack. Embroider around the edge of each ear with three strands of embroidery thread, using blanket stitch and leaving the top of the ear open. (For details of how to work the hand stitches, see pages 108–11.)

6

Stuff the ears lightly. Sew the ears to the head using three strands of embroidery thread – work blanket stitch along the top of the ear, catching the ear to the head at the same time.

7

Embroider the facial features using six strands of black embroidery thread. For the eyes, work French knots with three loops. Backstitch the mouth and nose using the photo as a guide.

8

To close the head, turn in 6mm ($\frac{1}{4}$in) and slipstitch the edges together. Attach the head to the body: take a double thickness of sewing thread and slipstitch the head to the body. Sew where the head meets the body, then repeat to make it extra secure. You don't need to flatten the head to the body at all – just sew where it is touching and the slipstitch will ensure that the stitches will not be seen.

instructions

9

Use the templates to cut out the pieces for the legs (see pages 106–7). Place the two pieces for each leg with right sides together. Pin, tack and machine-stitch with a 6mm (¼in) seam, leaving the top of the leg open. Turn right side out and stuff.

10

Slipstitch the legs to the body, turning in 6mm (¼in) at the top of the leg. Sew right around the edges, forming a circle. Secure the thread to the body under the leg to start, and finish the stitching just under the top of the leg.

If you think cream is a bit impractical for a toy, why not try making a less conventional sheep with a body in patterned fleece? For the head, make sure you use a pale patterned fabric so the features stand out.

When cutting out each pair of pieces for the ears, legs and tail, and the two pieces for the back of the head, one of the pieces needs to be reversed.

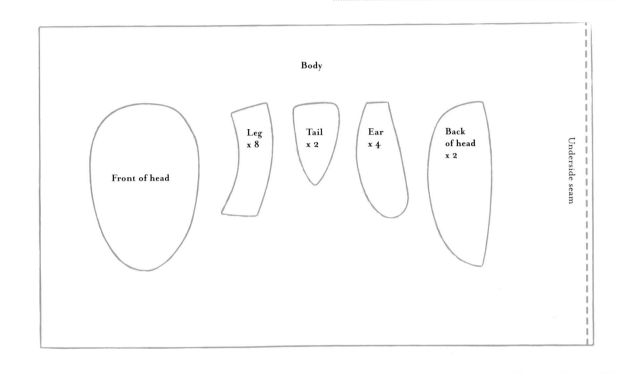

Body

Leg
x 8

Tail
x 2

Ear
x 4

Back
of head
x 2

Front of head

Underside seam

11

Use the template to cut out two tail pieces (see pages 106–7). Place the sections with wrong sides together and use three strands of embroidery thread to work blanket stitch around the edges, leaving the end where it will join the body open.

12

Stuff the tail lightly. Position it on the sheep's rear and sew on using three strands of embroidery thread – work blanket stitch along the top of the tail, catching the tail to the body at the same time.

13

Slipstitch the gap in the sheep's tummy to close it, making sure she is still well stuffed!

lucy
the elephant

Scraps of patterned cotton fabric (body/head/trunk)

Scraps of patterned cotton fabric (ears and legs)

Embroidery thread (black, red, blue and pink, or colours to suit)

Embroidery needle

Sewing machine

Sewing thread

Erasable fabric marker

Toy stuffing

Lucy is one of the trickier animals to make, due to her long trunk. I have used a very busy body fabric and a much simpler pattern for the legs and ears. You could try doing the opposite – it will produce a completely different effect.

instructions

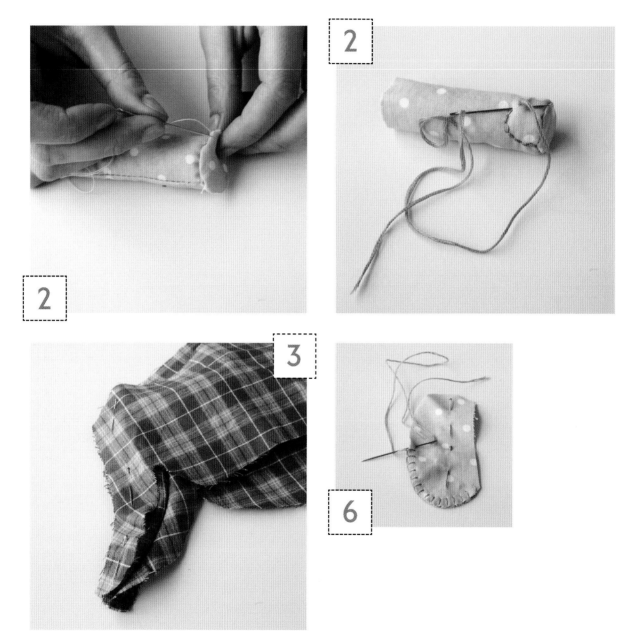

1

Use the templates to make a pattern and cut out the pieces for the elephant. Use a fabric marker to transfer pattern markings to the pieces (see pages 106–7).

2

Make the legs. Fold each piece in half, right sides together. Pin and tack along the long edge, then machine-stitch with a 6mm (¼in) seam. Turn right side out. Slipstitch the base of the foot to the bottom of the leg, turning in 6mm (¼in) as you go. (For details of how to work the hand stitches, see pages 108–11.) Stuff quite firmly.

Embroider the toes at the bottom of each leg, using six strands of embroidery thread and backstitch.

3

Make the body by placing the sections with right sides together, pinning, tacking and

machine-stitching with a 6mm (¼in) seam. Start by attaching the backbone/upper trunk section to the two side panels. Sew along the backbone and down the trunk; sew the underside of the trunk.

Lay the legs on the right side of the side panels as marked, with raw edges together and the legs lying on the body. The back seam of the legs should be facing the back of the body. Pin and tack in place. Make sure that the tops of the legs extend slightly above the body piece, to ensure that they will be caught securely in the seam.

Take the belly piece and pin and tack into position.

4

Machine-stitch around the belly gusset with a 6mm (¼in) seam, leaving it open where the belly gusset meets the backbone/trunk section at the elephant's rear end; the bottom end of the trunk is also left open. The area just under her trunk can be tricky to machine, but if a tiny gap remains, you can always slipstitch the edges together.

5

Turn the body the right way out and stuff through the rear end. Use a pencil to get the stuffing right down the trunk. Sew on the end of the trunk, using the same method as for the feet; before doing this, embroider two nostrils on the end piece – use three strands of embroidery thread and sew two little lines side by side for each nostril.

6

Place the two pieces for each ear with wrong sides together. Pin and tack. Embroider all the way around the edge of each ear with three strands of embroidery thread, using blanket stitch, and stuffing them lightly before finishing the row of stitching.

7

Position the ears on the head and attach with slipstitch, using three strands of embroidery thread and working through the blanket stitch.

instructions

Embroider the facial features using six strands of black embroidery thread. For the eyes, make French knots. Backstitch a mouth under the trunk.

Make the tail by cutting six strands of embroidery thread, about 20cm (8in) long, in different colours. Tie a knot in one end and then thread all six strands through a large-eyed needle and push it through the rear end of the elephant (from inside the body) where the tail is to go. Plait the tail to the required length, knot the end and trim off the excess.

10

Slipstitch the gap in the rear end to close it, adding more stuffing to the elephant first if necessary.

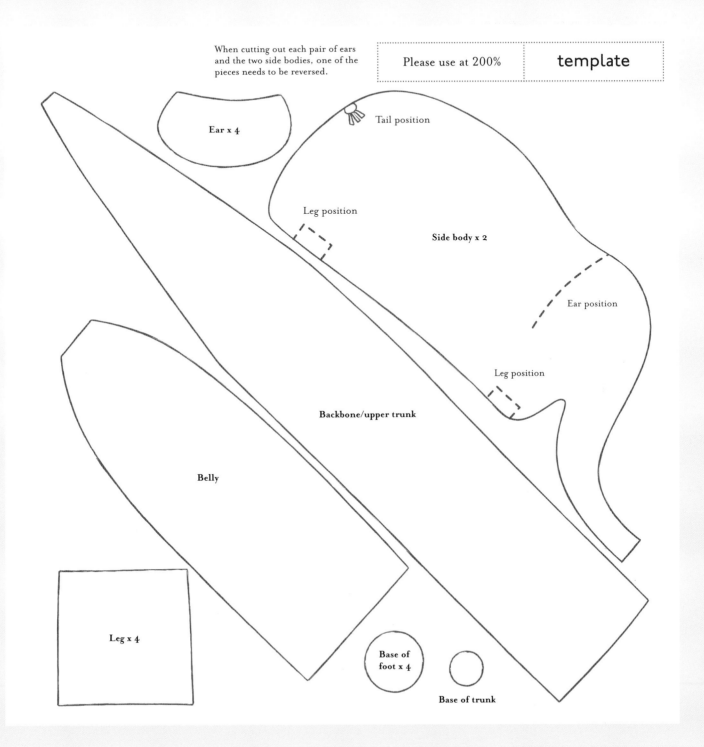

When cutting out each pair of ears
and the two side bodies, one of the
pieces needs to be reversed.

Please use at 200%

template

Ear x 4

Tail position

Leg position

Side body x 2

Ear position

Leg position

Backbone/upper trunk

Belly

Leg x 4

Base of
foot x 4

Base of trunk

luke
the monkey

Luke is full of fun: he will love chasing around with his owner and will make sure the pair of them don't get into too much trouble! The rest of the time he's happy to perch on a shelf or snuggle up for a nap.

instructions

Use the templates to make a pattern and cut out the pieces. Use a fabric marker to transfer pattern markings (see pages 106–7).

Make the arms, legs and tail. Pin front and back sections with right sides together, then tack. Machine-stitch the edges with a 6mm (¼in) seam, leaving the body end open. Turn right side out and stuff firmly.

For the ears, pin the front and back, wrong sides together. Tack. Using three strands of embroidery thread, sew together with blanket stitch, leaving the body end open. (For hand stitches, see pages 108–11.) Backstitch the shape of the inner ear on the front ear. Stuff the ears lightly.

Make the body. Pin the two pieces for the back with right sides together. Tack. Machine-stitch along the backbone with a 6mm (¼in) seam.

4

Lay the front body piece right side up. Lay the arms and legs on the body where marked, with raw edges together and the limbs lying on the body. Pin and tack in place. Make sure that the tops of the limbs extend slightly above the body piece, to ensure that they will be caught securely in the seam.

Follow the same procedure with the ears (the back of the ears should be uppermost).

Place the right side of the gusset on the right side of the front body piece, with raw edges together (and positioned over the legs). Pin and tack.

With right sides together, pin and tack the front of the body into position. Machine-stitch around the body with a 6mm (¼in) seam, as far as each side of the gusset. Stitch from the top of the gusset around the front body piece, trapping in the legs. Sew around the back gusset, leaving a gap for turning.

Turn the monkey right side out. Stuff him quite firmly.

6

Create the face. Draw around the template for the face shape on greaseproof paper. Cut it out and pin on the head. Backstitch the shape with six strands of embroidery thread. Sew a small cross for his tummy button.

7

Work the facial features in six strands of black embroidery thread. For the eyes, backstitch a small circle and then fill it with satin stitch. Sew two layers to make the eyes slightly raised. Backstitch the mouth and nose.

8

Add more stuffing if required, and slipstitch the gap in the gusset to close.

Slipstitch the tail to the body, turning in 6mm (¼in) at the top end. Sew right around the edges, forming a circle. Secure the thread to the body under the tail to start, and finish the stitching just under the top of the tail.

When cutting out each pair of
arms, legs and ears, one of the
pieces needs to be reversed.

Please use at 200%

template

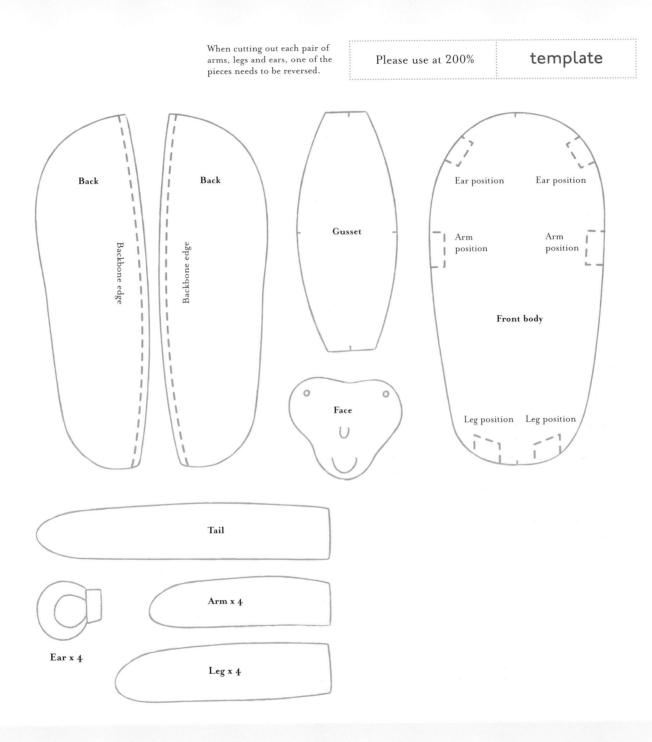

Back

Back

Backbone edge

Backbone edge

Gusset

Ear position   Ear position

Arm
position

Arm
position

Front body

Leg position   Leg position

Face

Tail

Ear x 4

Arm x 4

Leg x 4

animal book

You will need

Patterned cotton fabric:
0.25m x 114cm (^{1}/$_4$yd x 45in)
(book cover)

Soft white or cream fabric,
such as brushed cotton: 1m x
114cm (1yd x 45in) (pages)

White or cream fleece: 0.5m x
147cm (^{1}/$_2$yd x 58in) (stuffing
for pages)

Scraps of patterned cotton
fabrics (animals)

Double-sided fusible webbing
(such as Bondaweb)

Embroidery thread (various
colours)

Embroidery needle

Sewing machine with freehand
foot

Sewing thread

Erasable fabric marker

Iron-on transfer pen
(optional)

Ruler

This special picture book can be passed on from one generation to another and will be loved by all. The fabrics for the animals are mostly those used to make the toys; children will love to see their animal friends in this book.

instructions

Prepare the pages: cut seven squares of the soft fabric, 21 x 21cm (8¼ x 8¼in).

Make the animals. Transfer the templates to the webbing: place the webbing over the template, paper side up, and trace the lines. Cut out the shapes roughly. Place each shape, paper side up, on the wrong side of the appropriate fabric. Iron for 3–4 seconds (no steam). Cut out the shapes accurately.

Peel off the backing paper and lay the pieces, coated side down, on the front of the pages. Iron in place and leave to cool (see pages 106–7).

3

Using the freehand foot, machine-stitch carefully around each motif just inside the edge, and to highlight features. You can use an embroidery hoop if you wish. If you prefer to sew by hand, backstitch with sewing

thread. Alternatively, use three strands of embroidery thread and running stitch, or whipstitch the edges, or use blanket stitch. (For hand stitches, see pages 108–11.)

For the monkey's face, draw around the template on greaseproof paper. Cut it out and pin on the head. Backstitch around the shape with six strands of embroidery thread.

For the facial features, use black embroidery thread. Use all six strands for the sheep, pig and monkey and three strands for the other animals. Make French knots for the eyes on all the animals except the pig. Use satin stitch for the pig's eyes. If you prefer to have a drawn line to follow, use an erasable fabric marker or an iron-on transfer pen (see page 107).

Cut three squares of fabric for the book's cover, 21 x 21cm (8¼ x 8¼in). Decorate the front cover with paw shapes: transfer

the templates to webbing and on to the fabric, and fix to the cover as described for the animals. Using the freehand foot, machine-stitch around each motif just inside the edge.

6

Pin pairs of pages back to back. The front cover is pinned to the third square of cover fabric. The back cover is pinned to the last animal page. Embroider around each pair of pages, using three strands of embroidery thread and blanket stitch, and leaving the spine edge open.

Now cut five squares of fleece, 20 x 20cm (8 x 8in), to stuff the pages. Slot them in to give the pages extra thickness and make them easier for tiny hands to turn.

7

Stack up all the pages. Using a large-eyed needle and three strands of embroidery thread, sew along the spine with blanket stitch. Make sure that you catch in every page each time, and that the pages remain aligned.

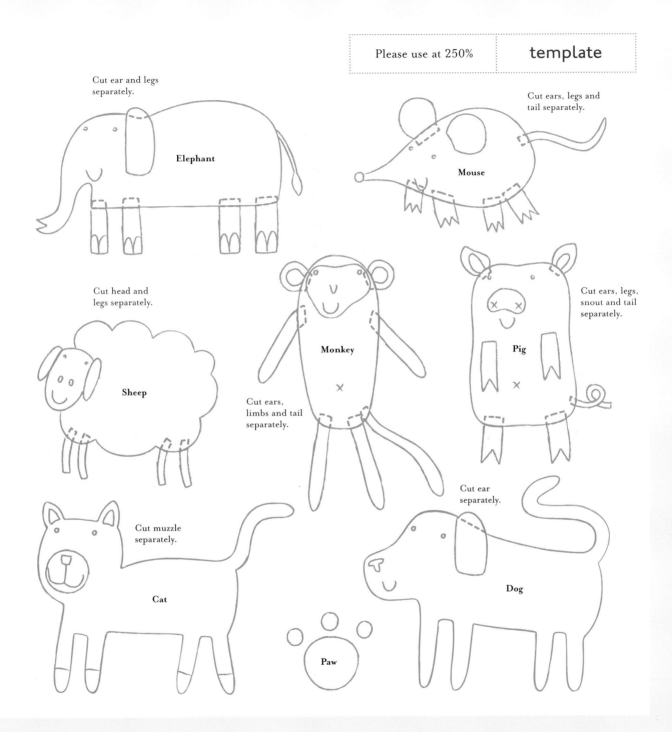

techniques

Using templates

Transferring templates

Printed templates provide the pattern pieces for each project. To transfer a template to fusible webbing, take a piece of webbing and place it over the template, paper side up. Draw around the shape. Cut out the shape very roughly, leaving a border around the edge.

For pattern pieces that do not require webbing, trace the template on to greaseproof paper and cut out. Lay it on the right side of the fabric (so you can see which part of the fabric's pattern lies in the motif) and pin. Cut round the shape, adding a seam allowance if necessary.

Reversing templates

Remember, when drawing directly on to double-sided fusible webbing, that the pattern piece will end up reversed in its final form (ironed on to fabric).

If you need to reverse a motif (for example to have an animal facing in the opposite direction), trace the template on to greaseproof paper and turn it over; use this new template in the same way as before.

Template details

Use the notches/lines on the templates as a guide for positioning legs, tails and ears. There are also letters and numbers to help match up parts.

All the templates allow for a 6mm ($^{1}/_{4}$in) seam. If you would prefer a larger seam to give you extra room when sewing, add an extra 6mm ($^{1}/_{4}$in) around the template as you cut it out.

Enlarging templates

If you need to enlarge (or reduce) a template, use a photocopier and just enter the percentage enlargement you need. Make sure that the machine hasn't distorted the image by stretching it.

Transferring designs to fabric

You may want to have a drawn image to embroider over, rather than doing it by eye – for example the features on an animal's face. You can either draw freehand with an erasable fabric marker, or transfer the details from a drawing with an iron-on transfer pen.

Erasable fabric markers

There are various types of markers – such as marking pencils that rub or wash out, water-erasable pens that wash out, and air-erasable pens where the lines you draw will vanish after a period of time.

Iron-on transfer pen or pencil

Bear in mind that some transfer pens produce a permanent image on fabric – check the manufacturer's instructions.

To use the transfer pen, put greaseproof paper over the template and trace the details on to it. (Remember that the image will be reversed when you iron it on, so if you want it the other way round, begin by tracing the details on to greaseproof with a normal pencil and then flip it over and draw over these lines with the transfer pen.) Place the image on the right side of the fabric and iron over it to transfer the lines to the fabric.

To position details accurately – such as facial features on a head – first trace the outline of the head in pencil on one side of the greaseproof paper, then turn it over and draw over the features with the transfer pen.

Using stabilizers

A stabilizer is a type of fabric that is used as a backing for embroidery, appliqué or other decorative needlework. It makes the surface fabric firmer and easier to work on, and ensures that it moves smoothly through a sewing machine when doing machine stitching. Used in appliqué, it allows you to cut out a solid motif that will not fray round the edges. There are various types, such as fusible, tear-away and water-soluble.

You can also stabilize a fabric while you work on it – by hand or machine – by putting it into an embroidery hoop. This holds the fabric flat and taut.

Double-sided fusible webbing

Double-sided fusible webbing, such as Vilene Bondaweb, allows you to trace a template directly on to the webbing, and transfer that shape to fabric. You then cut out the motif, which can be ironed on to the main part of the project.

Using double-sided fusible webbing

1 Trace the template motif on to the paper side of the webbing and cut it out roughly. (If you are making several motifs from the same fabric, draw them all near each other and cut them out as a group.)

2 Place the motif, coated side (glue side) down, on the wrong side of the motif fabric. Iron for 3–4 seconds (do not use steam) so the shape sticks to the fabric.

3 Cut out the motif accurately and peel off the backing paper.

4 Position the motif, right side up, on the right side of the main fabric piece. Cover with a damp cloth and iron on carefully, pressing down lightly and making sure you don't move the motif as you iron. Don't try to iron on all the motifs at once: one or two at a time is fine. Iron for about 10 seconds, until the motif has bonded with the main fabric piece. Be careful when checking that it has bonded, as it will still be hot.

5 Lay the fused parts flat and leave to cool.

Tear-away fusible stabilizer

Tear-away fusible stabilizer, such as Vilene Stitch 'n' Tear, may be ironed on to the back of a fabric piece that is to be covered in decorative needlework. When you have finished stitching, the stabilizer can be pulled away from the back of the work, even inside the area covered by a motif.

Hand stitches

Many of the projects feature stitches that are made by hand – either basic sewing stitches made in ordinary sewing thread, or decorative stitches worked in embroidery thread.

Starting and finishing stitching

For basic sewing, make several stitches on top of each other to secure the thread when you start. When using embroidery thread, knot the ends of the thread together – if you are working with all six strands, make a single knot; if using three strands, tie two knots, one on top of the other.

To finish, all you need to do is take the thread to the back of the fabric and sew over and over on the same spot about four times, catching in just a few threads of the fabric so it is hardly visible from the front. (If you are finishing off under a motif, just sew into the backing fabric and not the motif.) Alternatively, you can use the back of an embroidery stitch and sew over and over on it.

Sometimes you may want to make sure that finishing off stitches do not show at all on the front of the fabric, for example if you have been embroidering features on a stuffed animal. In this case you can 'lose' the end of the thread – just push the needle into the animal at your last stitch and bring it out as far away from that position as you can without losing the needle. Pull it slightly taut and cut off near the fabric, so when you let it go it will disappear into the animal and remains trapped in the stuffing.

Gathering

To gather by hand, secure the thread and make a basic running stitch along the area you need to gather, then pull up the stitches. Alternatively, start stitching with running stitch, leaving a tail of thread but not actually securing it – make sure you keep hold of the end. Then take both ends and pull to gather the fabric.

To gather by machine, set the stitch length selector to the longest possible stitch length. Secure the thread by stitching backwards for a few stitches, then stitch along the gathering line. (Or leave the end of the thread unsecured, as described for gathering by hand.)

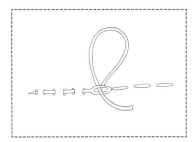

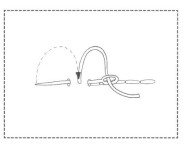

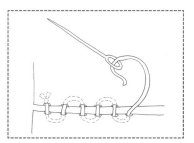

Running stitch

1. Knot the thread and bring the needle up through the back of the fabric.

2. Take a small stitch and push the needle back down through the fabric.

3. Repeat, trying to keep each stitch the same length and the gaps between them the same as the stitch lengths.

4. The diagram shows how to make several stitches at once by threading the needle in and out of the fabric before pulling the thread through.

Backstitch

1. Knot the thread and bring the needle up through the back of the fabric.

2. Take a small stitch behind where the needle exited and push the needle back down through the fabric.

3. Now take the needle back up through the fabric to the left of the first stitch, the same length away from the first exit hole as the previous stitch.

4. Repeat to make a neat, continuous line of stitches (on the underside of the work, the threads will overlap).

Slipstitch

Slipstitch is an almost invisible stitch used to provide a very neat finish. For example, when making a soft toy it is necessary to leave a gap in a seam to insert stuffing. To finish off, the turned-in edges of the seam are slipstitched together.

1. Make a knot in the thread and bring the needle through the seam (see diagram – the dotted lines are inside the fabric).

2. Then push the needle through the other seam, go along a bit and bring the needle out again. Repeat along the seam.

3. Remember to keep the stitches small, fairly close together and even.

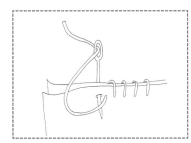

Whipstitch

For the projects in this book, a slightly irregular appearance is fine and adds to the charm.

Whipstitching two pieces of fabric together

1. Place the fabrics with wrong sides together. Make a knot in the thread and push the needle through the fabric from the wrong side, about 6mm ($\frac{1}{4}$in) from the raw edge of one fabric.

2. Take the thread over the raw edge and insert the needle through both pieces of fabric at a slight angle, again at 6mm ($\frac{1}{4}$in) from the raw edge. Repeat.

Whipstitching a motif to a fabric piece

1. Pin the wrong side of the motif to the right side of fabric. Use the same method as above, taking the stitch over the edge of the motif and down into the main fabric.

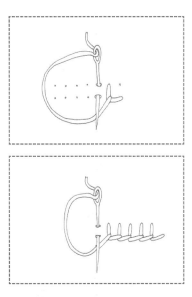

Blanket stitch

Blanket stitch is used to sew two pieces of fabric together, finishing and outlining the edge at the same time. It can be worked in embroidery thread as a decorative stitch, and in some projects is used to attach a motif.

1. Bring the thread out near the edge of the fabric. Then, without pulling tightly and referring to the diagram, push the needle through a certain distance across and down from the raw edge (however big you would like the stitch to be), allowing the thread to form into a loop behind the needle.

2. Pull the thread tightly to create the stitch.

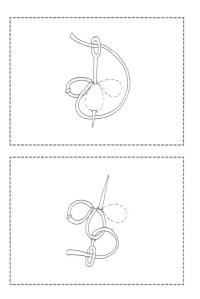

Lazy daisy stitch

1. Sew a small circle consisting of seven stitches. Then, working from the wrong side, bring the thread out to the right side between the first pair of stitches in the circle.

2. Form the thread into a loop the size of the petal and insert the needle where it last emerged (but do not pull tight).

3. Push the needle through to the right side, making it emerge at the outer end of the petal.

4. Make a small stitch over the end of the petal, pushing the needle through to the wrong side to secure the loop. Repeat to make seven petals.

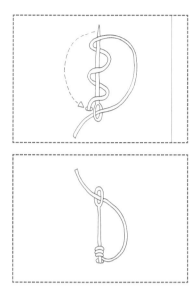

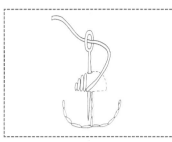

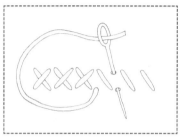

French knot

1. Knot the end of the thread and bring the needle through to the right side of the fabric.

2. Twist the thread around the needle two or three times. Holding the thread taut, push the needle back into the fabric very close to where it exited.

3. With the tip of the needle in the fabric, slide the knot down the needle (keep the thread taut).

4. Push the needle through to the back of the fabric; hold the thread down with your thumb so you can see the knot forming. Keep pulling until the thread goes through the knot. Pull tight. This stitch may take practice.

Satin stitch

Satin stitch is used to fill small areas to give a smooth, solid surface. I often go over my satin stitch twice, and for a large area I tend to sew smaller stitches over the top in other directions: this is not essential but I find it builds up the area nicely and holds the satin stitch in place. You can do this on small areas too, as the satin stitch used in the projects in this book is purely to build up an area of colour rather than to look nice as a technique.

1. Knot the thread and bring the needle through to the front of the fabric.

2. Use backstitch to create an outline of the shape to be filled.

3. Beginning at one end of the shape, start to fill it by working a series of parallel stitches that butt up against one another.

Cross-stitch

1. Knot the thread and bring the needle through to the front of the fabric.

2. Work a line of stitches slanting to the left. At the end of the line, bring the needle out to the front of the fabric at what will be the bottom left-hand corner of the cross. Work a line of stitches slanting to the right, to form a row of crosses.

3. To work a single random cross-stitch, make a left-slanting stitch covered by a right-slanting stitch, as described above.

Using a sewing machine

You will need a sewing machine for basic operations such as seaming together pattern pieces, and to create decorative stitching.

Free-motion sewing

For lots of the projects, you will need a freehand foot to allow you to do free-motion sewing. This spring-loaded foot 'hops', allowing you to manoeuvre the fabric easily to stitch curves and other shapes. You can purchase one from a haberdashery department or a sewing machine shop. Check in the store to find out which foot will fit on your sewing machine.

Free-motion stitch is rather like drawing with a sewing machine, and is very simple once you get the hang of it. You may need to practise before sewing something tiny. Part of the charm of free-motion stitching is that you can create lines that look quite naive yet are still very skilful and effective. For some pieces you may find it easier to use an embroidery hoop to hold the fabric. It will give you more control and prevent the fabric from being dragged down into the machine. It will also make it safer for you and ensure that you don't get your hand caught by the needle.

Stitching around a motif

1 Attach the foot and lower the feed dogs on the machine (these help drag fabric through the machine, which you don't want when you're doing free-motion sewing).

2 Stitch around the motifs, a little way in from the edge, at whatever speed you like. The key to producing a neat effect is to move the fabric round slowly but have the needle working at a fast pace.

3 To start and finish stitching, just go back and forth over the stitching line a couple of times. Alternatively, leave some thread hanging from both ends and finish it off by hand afterwards.

Seams

The seam allowances included in most of the project templates are 6mm ($\frac{1}{4}$in), but if you prefer to have a larger seam to give you extra room when sewing, you can add extra around the template as you cut it out. (For larger pieces of fabric, there are seam allowances of 1.5cm [$\frac{1}{2}$in].) Stitch the seam, press it and then trim it to 6mm ($\frac{1}{4}$in).

To ensure that a curved seam lies flat when the item is turned right side out, cut little triangular notches of fabric out of the seam allowance.

Author's Acknowledgments

I have many people to thank for the completion of my book. First, I would like to thank everyone at Anova Books for making this book possible and for all their help along the way. A special thanks to Miriam, Nihal, Fiona, and Louise and also to Christina for the wonderful photographs. I would also like to thank my family for their constant support and for believing in me. A big thanks also goes to my friends for their great interest and encouragement in everything I do. Finally, I would like to thank Coats Crafts UK for providing a lot of the fabrics and threads I used in the projects and also for giving me the experience at designing and writing craft projects.

The publisher would like to thank our models Valerio Thompson and Lara Yun Moeller.

Photography by Christina Wilson.